Getting Down to Brass Tacks

Getting Down to Brass Tacks

A No-Nonsense Guide to Living a Focused, Purposeful Life

Robert T. Yarborough

Pranava Books

Getting Down to Brass Tacks: A No-Nonsense Guide to Living a Focused, Purposeful Life

Publisher's Cataloging-in-Publication Data

Yarborough, Robert T., 1960-
Getting Down to Brass Tacks: A No-Nonsense Guide to Living a Focused, Purposeful Life / by Robert T. Yarborough.
    —First edition.
    p. cm.
    Includes bibliographical references.
    ISBN: 979-8-9912582-0-3

1. Self-Help. 2. Personal Growth. 3. Time Management. 4. Motivation. 5. Focus. 6. Values.

BF637.S4 Y37 2024
158.1 YAR 2024
Library of Congress Control Number: 2024918688

10 9 8 7 6 5 4 3 2 1

Dedication

To the weight on my heart and the joy in my soul — my children
Savannah, Sydney, and Sage.

My greatest hope is that you live a life that truly matters,
is grounded in purpose, and is filled with love.

Contents

Author's Preface

"Do not wait; the time will never be 'just right.' Start where you stand, and work with whatever tools you may have at your command."
— *Napoleon Hill*

In today's world we're constantly bombarded with information, opportunities, and distractions that pull us in every direction. In the midst of this chaos, it's no wonder that many of us struggle to find a sense of purpose and fulfillment.

That's where this book comes in.

Getting Down to Brass Tacks was born out of a simple idea: What if we stripped away all the noise and focused only on what truly matters? What if we lived our lives with intention, making choices that align with our deepest values and long-term goals? How much more meaningful and fulfilling would our lives be?

This book isn't about offering you a quick fix or a one-size-fits-all solution. Instead, it's about helping you cut through the clutter and get to the heart of what really matters in your life. It's about giving you the tools to live a life that's focused, intentional, and aligned with your core values.

The principles and strategies you'll find in this book are practical and actionable. They're designed to be used every day, in the real world, where distractions are constant and time is always in short supply. Whether you're looking to improve your personal life, advance your career, or simply find more peace and clarity, the tools in this book can help you get there.

As you read through these pages, I encourage you to think about how each principle applies to your own life. Reflect on your core values, reassess your priorities, and make the decision to focus on what truly matters. The journey won't always be easy, but I can promise you this: It will be worth it.

Thank you for picking up this book and choosing to embark on this journey. I'm excited to see where it takes you.

‡ ‡ ‡

Introduction

The Essence of Brass Tacks

"Simplicity is the ultimate sophistication."
— Leonardo da Vinci

Exploring the Metaphor of Brass Tacks

Let's skip the small talk and get right to it: If you want to achieve real results, you must focus on what truly matters—cutting through the noise and getting down to the brass tacks. The phrase "brass tacks" has been around for a while, and it's often used when someone wants to strip away all the unnecessary details and get to the core of an issue. In this book, that's precisely what we will do—focus on the essentials that will help you live a purposeful, focused life.

When we talk about "brass tacks," we're talking about getting to the foundation, the underlying truths that count. When you're overwhelmed with tasks, obligations, and endless distractions, it's easy to get lost in the chaos. The concept of brass tacks urges you to sift through the clutter and identify what's truly important. It's about simplifying, prioritizing, and making decisions that align with your core values.

The Significance of This Metaphor in Leading a Purposeful, Focused Life

Living a life focused on what truly matters isn't just a nice idea—it's essential for your well-being and success. The metaphor of brass tacks is significant because it is a constant reminder to strip away the excess and concentrate on what will move the needle in your life. Whether it's your career, relationships, or personal growth, getting down to brass tacks means you're not wasting time on trivialities. Instead, you're honing in on the actions and decisions that will lead to tangible outcomes.

In today's world, where distractions are endless, and information overload is the norm, the ability to focus on the essentials is more valuable than ever. Think of it this way: every time you make a decision, you have the opportunity to choose whether you will focus on what matters or get sidetracked by the noise. The *Brass Tacks* approach helps you consistently choose the former.

Setting the Stage for a Comprehensive Guide to Living with Intention

This book is a practical guide to help you refocus your life. We'll cover everything from identifying your core values to implementing daily habits that support a life of purpose and intention. Each chapter builds on the last, providing you with the tools and strategies to cut through the distractions and focus on what truly matters.

As we move forward, remember that this isn't about perfection—it's about progress. The goal is to equip you with a mindset and a set of practices to help you make more intentional daily choices. By the end of this book, you'll understand what's important to you and how to align your actions with those priorities.

Why Focus Matters

The Impact of Distraction and Clutter in Modern Life

Distractions are everywhere, from the constant barrage of notifications on your phone to the endless stream of information online. It's easy to get overwhelmed and lose sight of what really matters. The demand for our attention is relentless, and the consequences are significant. Distraction not only eats away at our time but also diminishes our ability to think clearly, make decisions, and ultimately live a life of purpose.

Clutter, both physical and mental, compounds this problem. It's not just about having too much stuff in your living space; it's about the mental clutter that comes from juggling too many tasks, ideas, and obligations. When your mind is cluttered, your energy is scattered. You're more likely to feel stressed, anxious, and unable to focus on what's important. This constant distraction and clutter keeps you stuck in a cycle of busyness without real progress.

To put it bluntly, if you're not managing your focus, you're letting the distractions and clutter of life control you. And that's no way to live a meaningful, productive life.

Benefits of Honing in on What Truly Matters

So, why should you care about honing in on what truly matters? The answer is simple: focus is the key to achieving meaningful results in any area of life. You start to see real progress when you're clear on your priorities and consistently direct your energy toward them. This isn't just about crossing things off your to-do list; it's about making choices that align with your values and long-term goals.

When you focus on what truly matters, several things happen:

Increased Productivity. You accomplish more in less time because you're not wasting energy on distractions or trivial tasks. Your efforts are concentrated on actions that have a real impact.

Improved Decision-Making. With a clear understanding of your priorities, making decisions becomes easier. You can quickly assess whether an opportunity or task is worth your time based on whether it aligns with your goals.

Greater Fulfillment. A deep sense of satisfaction comes from knowing you're spending your time and energy on things that truly matter. This leads to a more fulfilling life because your actions align with your values.

Reduced Stress. Eliminating unnecessary distractions and clutter creates more mental space. This reduction in cognitive overload[1] leads to lower stress levels and a clearer mind.

In short, focusing on what matters helps you cut through the noise and live a life that's more productive and aligned with who you are and what you want to achieve.

How This Book Will Guide You Through the Process of Refocusing Your Life

This book isn't just another self-help manual filled with vague advice. It's a practical guide designed to help you systematically refocus your life on what truly matters. Throughout the chapters, you'll find straightforward strategies and actionable steps to help you declutter your mind, clarify your priorities, and build habits that support a focused, intentional life.

Here's how we'll do it:

Identifying Your Core Values. We'll start by helping you define what's most important to you. This is the foundation for everything else in the book. Once you're clear on your values, you can start making decisions that align with them.

Setting Priorities. Next, we'll dive into how to set and maintain priorities in a world full of distractions. You'll learn techniques for

---

[1] Cognitive overload refers to a state in which an individual's working memory is overwhelmed by the amount of information they are attempting to process, leading to reduced comprehension, decision-making, and performance.

staying focused on the things that matter most, even when life gets hectic.

Developing a Focused Mindset. We'll explore the mental shifts needed to maintain focus over the long term. This includes strategies for managing stress, staying disciplined, and cultivating resilience.

Practical Applications. Finally, we'll cover practical applications of focus in various areas of your life, from work to relationships to personal growth. You'll learn how to apply the principles of focus to create real, lasting change.

By the end of this book, you'll have a clear roadmap for living a life centered on what truly matters. You'll have the tools and mindset to eliminate distractions, overcome challenges, and make meaningful progress toward your goals. This isn't about making dramatic changes overnight; it's about making steady, intentional shifts that lead to a more focused and fulfilling life.

Let's get down to brass tacks and start living a life that truly matters.

1

Identifying What Truly Matters

"It is not the length of life, but the depth."
— *Ralph Waldo Emerson*

Clarifying Your Core Values

If you want to live a focused, intentional life, you must start by clarifying your core values. These are the principles that define who you are and guide your decisions. Without a clear understanding of your values, it's easy to get pulled in a hundred different directions, chasing goals that don't truly resonate with you. But when you're clear on your values, you have a reliable compass that helps you navigate life's challenges and opportunities with purpose and clarity.

Importance of Core Values in Living a Focused Life

Core values are the fundamental beliefs that shape your attitudes, behaviors, and decisions. They're the "brass tacks" of your identity—the non-negotiable principles that matter most to you. Whether it's integrity, family, growth, or health, these values are the foundation upon which you build your life.

Living in alignment with your core values is crucial for several reasons.

Consistency in Decision-Making. When you know what's important to you, making decisions becomes easier. You can quickly determine whether a choice aligns with your values, helping you stay on track and avoid unnecessary distractions (Schwartz, 2012).

Increased Satisfaction. Aligning your actions with your values leads to greater fulfillment. You're not just going through the motions; you're living an authentic and meaningful life (Covey, 1989).

Resilience in Difficult Times. Core values provide a strong foundation during challenging moments. When you're clear on what matters most, you can weather storms with a sense of purpose, knowing that your decisions are grounded in your beliefs (Dweck, 2006).

Identify and Articulate Your Core Values

Identifying your core values isn't something you can do passively. It requires introspection and honest reflection. Here's a simple exercise to help you clarify your values.

Reflect on Peak Experiences. Think about moments when you felt pleased, proud, or fulfilled. What was happening? Who were you with? What values were being honored during these times? Write down the common themes.

Examine Your Daily Choices. Look at how you spend your time and money—these are often strong indicators of what you value. Growth might be your core value if you're constantly investing in education. If you prioritize time with family, relationships could be central to your values.

Prioritize Your List. Once you've identified several potential values, rank them in order of importance. This will help you determine which are core to your identity and which are secondary.

Test Your Values. Imagine scenarios where you must make tough choices. For example, if family and career rank high on your list, what would you choose if the two conflict? Testing your values in hypothetical situations helps clarify which ones are non-negotiable.

Articulate Your Values. Once you've narrowed your list, write a brief statement for each core value that explains why it's important to you and how it influences your life. This step is crucial because it forces you to be specific and intentional about your values.

Individuals Who Aligned Their Lives with Their Values

Examining real-world examples can provide powerful insights into how aligning with core values leads to meaningful and impactful lives. Let's look at how some notable individuals have exemplified this alignment.

Case Study 1. Steve Jobs – Innovation and Simplicity

Steve Jobs, co-founder of Apple Inc., built his career and company around the core values of innovation and simplicity. Jobs believed in creating products that were not only technologically advanced but also intuitively simple and aesthetically pleasing. This commitment is evident in Apple's product designs and user interfaces, prioritizing ease of use and elegant design (Isaacson, 2011).

Jobs' focus on these values led to revolutionary products like the iPhone and iPad, transforming multiple industries and setting new standards for technology and design. By steadfastly adhering to his core values, Jobs was able to drive innovation and create a lasting legacy in the tech world. As Jobs once said, "Simple can be harder than complex. You have to work hard to get your thinking clean to make it simple" (Isaacson, 2011, p. 343).

Case Study 2. Malala Yousafzai – Education and Equality

Malala Yousafzai's life is a testament to her unwavering commitment to education and gender equality. Growing up in Pakistan, Malala advocated for girls' right to education in the face of oppressive regimes that sought to deny this fundamental right. Even after surviving an assassination attempt by the Taliban, she continued her activism on a global scale (Yousafzai & Lamb, 2013).

Her dedication led to the establishment of the Malala Fund, which provides education opportunities to girls worldwide. At 17, she became the youngest-ever Nobel Peace Prize laureate, recognized for her struggle against the suppression of children and young people and the right to education (Nobel Prize, 2014). Malala's alignment with her core values has inspired millions and brought significant attention and resources to the cause of educational equality.

Case Study 3. Elon Musk – Sustainability and Exploration

Elon Musk has consistently demonstrated a commitment to the values of sustainability and exploration throughout his entrepreneurial endeavors. Musk aims to accelerate the world's transition to sustainable energy with Tesla Motors by producing high-performing and environmentally friendly electric vehicles. Similarly, through SpaceX, Musk seeks to advance space exploration and make humanity a multi-planetary species, reflecting his belief in pushing the boundaries of what's possible and ensuring the long-term survival of humankind (Vance, 2015).

By embedding these core values into his companies' missions, Musk has achieved remarkable business success and driven significant progress in renewable energy and space technology.

These case studies illustrate how identifying and steadfastly adhering to one's core values can lead to profound personal fulfillment and transformative impact. Whether innovating technology, advocating for education, or advancing sustainability, aligning actions with deeply held beliefs enables individuals to focus their efforts effectively and achieve extraordinary outcomes.

Clarifying your core values lays the groundwork for a focused, intentional life. It is the first step in cutting through the noise and getting down to the brass tacks of what truly matters.

Setting Life Priorities

Now that you've clarified your core values, the next step is to set your life priorities. Priorities are essentially the areas of your life that demand your attention and energy and should align closely with your values. When your priorities reflect your values, you're more likely to live a balanced, meaningful, and satisfying life. Let's dive into how to make that happen.

The Relationship Between Values and Priorities

Your values and priorities are deeply interconnected. Values are the principles you hold dear, while priorities are the tangible expressions of those values in your day-to-day life. For example, if one of your core values is family, spending quality time with your loved ones should be a top priority. If personal growth is a value, dedicating time to learning and self-improvement must be prioritized (Covey, 1989).

Think of values as your guiding stars—they give you direction. Priorities, however, are your actions and commitments that keep you on that path. When your priorities are aligned with your values, you're more likely to make decisions that bring you closer to your goals and create a sense of harmony in your life (Schwartz, 2012).

Techniques for Ranking and Balancing Life Priorities

Ranking and balancing your priorities can be challenging, especially when life pulls you in multiple directions. Here are some techniques to help you determine what deserves your focus.

Identify Your Key Life Areas. Start by identifying the main areas of your life that require attention—these might include family, career, health, finances, personal growth, and social connections. These are your broad categories for setting priorities.

Link Each Area to a Core Value. Link each key area to one of your core values. This helps ensure that your priorities are rooted in what truly matters to you. For example, if "health" is a key area, it might link to a core value of well-being or vitality (Rokeach, 1973).

Rank Your Priorities. Once you've linked your key areas to your values, rank them in order of importance. This isn't about deciding what's universally important but what's most important to you now. Be honest with yourself—what do you need to focus on right now to feel aligned with your values?

> **Example.** If family, health, and career are your top three priorities, decide which needs the most attention today, this week, or this month. Your ranking can change over time, so revisit it regularly.

Balance Your Priorities. Balancing priorities doesn't mean giving equal time to everything; it means giving the right amount of time to the right things. Use time management tools like time blocking or the Eisenhower Matrix (urgent vs. important) to help allocate your time effectively (Eisenhower, 1954).

Time Blocking. Dedicate specific blocks of time to your top priorities. For instance, block out time in the morning for personal growth (e.g., reading or learning) and the evening for family activities.

Eisenhower Matrix. This tool helps you decide what needs immediate attention (urgent and important), what you can schedule for later (important but not urgent), what to delegate (urgent but not important), and what to eliminate (neither urgent nor important).

Be Flexible. Life happens, and priorities can shift. The key is to stay flexible and adapt as needed without losing sight of your core values. If a new opportunity or challenge arises, assess how it fits your current priorities and adjust accordingly (Dweck, 2006).

How to Make Decisions That Reflect Your True Priorities

Making decisions that reflect your true priorities requires intentionality and a clear sense of what's most important to you. Here's a straightforward process to guide you.

Pause and Reflect. Before making a decision, pause and reflect on how it aligns with your priorities. Ask yourself, "Does this choice bring me closer to or further away from what I value most?" (Kahneman, 2011).

Consider the Long-Term Impact. Consider how this decision will affect your life in the long run. Will it support your long-term goals and values, or is it a short-term distraction?

Use the 80/20 Rule. Also known as the Pareto Principle, the 80/20 rule suggests that 80% of your results come from 20% of your efforts. Focus on the 20% of activities that impact your priorities most (Koch, 1998).

Say No When Necessary. One of the most challenging but most important aspects of setting priorities is learning to say no. If a decision or opportunity doesn't align with your top priorities, it's okay to decline. This frees up your time and energy for what truly matters (Sinek, 2009).

Review and Reassess Regularly. Life and your priorities are dynamic. Make it a habit to review your priorities regularly—monthly, quarterly, or even annually. This practice helps you stay aligned with your values and ensures that your daily actions reflect your priorities (Covey, 1989).

By setting and living according to your priorities, you create a life that's not only more focused but also more fulfilling. Your energy is directed toward what truly matters, allowing you to achieve your goals with clarity and purpose.

Remember, setting priorities isn't about doing everything—it's about doing the right things. Focus on what aligns with your core values, and you'll find that life becomes less about juggling tasks and more about making meaningful progress.

Eliminating the Non-Essential

Now that you've identified your core values and set your life priorities, it's time to tackle one of the most crucial steps in living a focused, intentional life, eliminating the non-essential. In a world overflowing with distractions, unnecessary obligations, and endless noise, eliminating what doesn't matter is essential for staying on track and aligning with your true priorities.

Identifying What Detracts from What Matters Most

Distractions come in many forms—some are obvious, like spending too much time on social media. Others are more subtle, such as unnecessary obligations or saying yes to things that don't serve your goals. To live a life focused on what truly matters, you must first identify these distractions and obligations that pull you away from your core values.

Here are some common distractions and obligations that might be taking up more of your time and energy than they deserve.

Digital Distractions. Endless scrolling on social media, binge-watching TV shows, and constantly checking emails or notifications are prime examples of digital distractions that eat away at your time without adding value to your life (Newport, 2016).

Unnecessary Obligations. These are tasks or commitments you've taken on out of habit, guilt, or social pressure rather than because they align with your values. This could include attending meetings that don't require your presence, volunteering for activities that don't resonate with your goals, or maintaining relationships that drain your energy (McKeown, 2014).

Busywork. Busywork refers to tasks that make you feel productive but don't contribute to your priorities. This might include reorganizing your desk for the third time this week, responding to non-urgent emails, or attending meetings with no apparent purpose (Drucker, 1967).

Mental Clutter. Mental clutter includes negative thought patterns, unresolved issues, and unfinished tasks that occupy your mind and prevent you from focusing on what's important. This can be just as draining as physical clutter, if not more so (Brown, 2010).

To eliminate these distractions, take an honest inventory of your daily activities. Track how you spend your time for a week and then assess which activities align with your core values and which don't. This exercise will give you a clear picture of where your time and energy are going and where you need to make adjustments.

Strategies for Decluttering Your Life Physically and Mentally

Decluttering your life involves more than just cleaning out your closet. It's about removing anything that doesn't serve your highest priorities, whether it's physical clutter, mental clutter, or time-wasting activities. Here are some strategies to help you declutter effectively.

Physical Decluttering.

Simplify Your Environment. Start with your physical space. Clear out items you no longer use, need, or love. A cluttered environment can lead to a cluttered mind, making it harder to focus on your priorities (Kondo, 2014).

Adopt the "One In, One Out" Rule. For every new item you bring into your space, eliminate something else. This helps maintain a clutter-free environment and prevents the accumulation of unnecessary stuff (Becker, 2013).

Create Dedicated Spaces. Organize your space to support your priorities. For example, if learning and personal growth are essential to you, create a dedicated reading or study area that's free from distractions.

Mental Decluttering.

Practice Mindfulness. Mindfulness is a powerful tool for clearing mental clutter. It helps you stay present and focused, reducing the impact of distractions and negative thought patterns. Set aside a few minutes each day to practice mindfulness or meditation (Kabat-Zinn, 1994).

Resolve Unfinished Business. Unresolved issues, whether they're personal or professional, can take up mental space and drain your energy. Make a plan to address these issues, whether that means having a difficult conversation, completing a lingering task, or letting go of something that no longer serves you (Brown, 2018).

Limit Information Intake. Today's world is constantly bombarded us with information. Be selective about what you consume—news, social media, or other content—and focus on what truly adds value to your life (McKeown, 2014).

Time Decluttering.

Audit Your Time. Just as you would with physical items, audit your time to identify activities that don't align with your priorities. This might include meetings, social events, or hobbies that no longer bring you joy or value (Covey, 1989).

Use Time-Blocking. Time-blocking[1] is a simple yet effective way to ensure your day reflects your priorities. You can prevent distractions from taking over by dedicating specific time blocks to essential tasks (Newport, 2016).

---

[1] Time blocking is a productivity technique where specific blocks of time are allocated for particular tasks or activities throughout the day. This method helps individuals focus on one task at a time, minimizing distractions and promoting deep work.

Schedule Downtime. It's important to schedule time for relaxation. Downtime is necessary for recharging your energy and maintaining mental clarity, so make sure it's part of your routine (Brown, 2010).

The Power of Saying No

One of the most powerful tools in your arsenal for eliminating the non-essential is the ability to say no. Saying no isn't about being selfish or uncooperative; it's about protecting your time and energy so that you can focus on what truly matters.

Here's how to harness the power of saying no.

Know Your Priorities. When you're clear on your priorities, it becomes easier to say no to anything that doesn't align with them. If an opportunity or request doesn't support your goals or values, it's okay to decline (Sinek, 2009).

Be Direct and Honest. Be direct and honest when saying no. You don't need to provide a lengthy explanation—simply stating that you're focusing on other commitments or that it doesn't align with your current priorities is enough (Covey, 1989).

Practice Saying No. If saying no feels uncomfortable, start by practicing in low-stakes situations. As you become more confident, you'll find it easier to say no when it counts (McKeown, 2014).

Offer Alternatives. If you feel compelled to help but can't commit, offer an alternative solution. For example, you might suggest someone else who's better suited for the task or offer to help at a later time when it fits your schedule.

Recognize the Long-Term Benefits. Remember that saying no today allows you to say yes to the things that truly matter in the long run. Whenever you say no to a distraction or unnecessary obligation, you make space for priorities aligning with your core values (Sinek, 2009).

By eliminating the non-essential, you free up time, energy, and mental space to focus on what truly matters. This is a critical step in living a life of purpose and intention. When you remove distractions, declutter your life, and learn to say no, you create a clear path toward achieving your goals and living in alignment with your values.

2

Building a Focused Mindset

"You have power over your mind—not outside events.
Realize this, and you will find strength."
— *Marcus Aurelius*

The Psychology of Focus

Focus isn't just about willpower; it's about understanding how your mind works and leveraging that knowledge to your advantage. If you want to master the art of focus, you need to grasp why it's so challenging and what you can do to enhance your concentration and mental clarity.

Why Focus Is Challenging

The human brain is wired for novelty. Evolution has favored a mind that's constantly scanning for new information and potential threats. This was great for our ancestors who needed to survive in the wild, but in today's world, it means that our brains are easily distracted by the constant barrage of stimuli—emails, notifications, social media, and so on. This is known as "attentional bias[1]," where your brain prioritizes new and interesting information over the task at hand (Anderson et al., 2011).

Another factor is "cognitive load[2]," which refers to the amount of mental effort used in the working memory. When your cognitive load is high—due to multitasking, stress, or information overload—your ability to focus diminishes (Sweller, 1988). Essentially, the more you try to juggle, the less effective you become at any one task.

Finally, there's the issue of "decision fatigue[3]." As you make decisions throughout the day, your mental energy depletes, making it harder to focus on tasks requiring sustained attention (Baumeister et al., 2000). This is why tasks that require deep concentration are often best tackled earlier in the day when your mental energy is at its peak.

Cognitive Techniques for Enhancing Concentration and Mental Clarity

Now that you understand why focus is challenging, let's talk about what you can do to improve it. Here are some practical cognitive techniques to enhance your concentration and mental clarity.

Single-Tasking. Multitasking might seem productive, but it's a focus killer. Studies have shown that multitasking reduces efficiency and cognitive performance (Rosen, 2008). Instead, practice single-tasking—focus on one task at a time, giving it your full attention before moving on to the next.

---

[1] Attentional bias refers to the cognitive tendency to focus on specific stimuli or information while neglecting others, often influenced by personal emotions, experiences, or concerns.

[2] Cognitive load refers to the amount of mental effort being used in the working memory. It plays a critical role in learning and information processing, as excessive cognitive load can hinder understanding and retaining new information.

[3] Decision fatigue refers to the deteriorating quality of decisions made by an individual after a long session of decision-making. As people make more decisions throughout the day, their ability to make effective choices decreases.

The Pomodoro Technique.[1]   This time management method involves working for 25 minutes, followed by a 5-minute break. After four cycles, take a longer break. This technique helps manage cognitive load by breaking work into manageable intervals, reducing the risk of burnout, and maintaining high levels of focus throughout the day (Cirillo, 2006).

Mind Mapping.[2]   Mind Mapping can help clarify your thoughts and organize information visually when faced with complex tasks or projects. This technique reduces cognitive load by externalizing information organization, allowing you to see the big picture and focus on what's most important (Buzan, 2006).

Eliminate Distractions.   Identify your biggest distractions and find ways to eliminate or minimize them. This could involve turning off notifications, setting boundaries with colleagues or family members, or creating a dedicated workspace free from interruptions. Reducing distractions lowers cognitive load and helps maintain focus.

Chunking Information.   Break down information into smaller, more manageable chunks. This is particularly useful when learning new material or tackling large projects. Chunking helps the brain process and retain information more efficiently, making it easier to maintain focus (Miller, 1956).

The Role of Mindfulness in Maintaining Focus

Mindfulness is more than just a buzzword; it's a scientifically supported practice that can significantly enhance your ability to focus. Mindfulness involves paying attention to the present moment without judgment,

---

[1] The Pomodoro Technique is a time management method developed by Francesco Cirillo in the late 1980s. It involves breaking work into intervals, traditionally 25 minutes in length, separated by short breaks. This approach is designed to improve focus and productivity.

[2] Mind mapping is a visual thinking tool that helps structure information, enabling better analysis, comprehension, and idea generation. It involves creating a diagram with a central concept, with related ideas branching out in a non-linear manner.

which helps you become more aware of when your mind starts to wander and brings it back to the task at hand (Kabat-Zinn, 1994).

Here's how mindfulness can help you maintain focus.

Increased Awareness. Practicing mindfulness makes you more attuned to your thoughts and feelings. This awareness lets you notice when your focus starts to drift and gently bring your attention back to the task. It's about developing the skill to refocus quickly rather than berating yourself for losing focus in the first place.

Reduced Stress and Anxiety. Mindfulness has been shown to reduce stress and anxiety, which are major contributors to cognitive load and distraction. By managing these emotions, you create a mental environment that's more conducive to sustained focus (Hölzel et al., 2011).

Enhanced Cognitive Flexibility. Mindfulness practice has been associated with improved cognitive flexibility, the ability to switch between different tasks and thought processes smoothly. This flexibility is crucial when shifting focus between tasks without losing productivity (Moore & Malinowski, 2009).

Daily Mindfulness Practice. Incorporate short mindfulness exercises into your daily routine, such as focusing on your breath for a few minutes each morning or practicing mindful walking. These practices train your brain to stay present and focused, making applying this mindset to more demanding tasks easier.

Understanding how your mind works, applying cognitive techniques, and incorporating mindfulness into your daily routine can enhance your ability to focus, reduce distractions, and maintain mental clarity. This is the foundation of a focused mindset, allowing you to cut through the noise and concentrate on what truly matters.

Cultivating Mental Resilience

To stay focused on what truly matters, you need more than just concentration—you need mental resilience. Life throws challenges at you, and your ability to handle them without losing focus sets you apart. Mental resilience isn't just about bouncing back from setbacks; it's about maintaining your composure and clarity even when things get tough.

Mental Toughness and Resilience in the Face of Challenges

Mental toughness is the ability to stay strong in the face of adversity. It's about pushing through discomfort, staying committed to your goals, and not letting setbacks derail you. Here's how you can build mental toughness.

Embrace Discomfort. Growth doesn't happen in your comfort zone. Seek out challenges that push you beyond your limits, whether taking on a new project at work or setting a challenging personal goal. Regularly exposing yourself to discomfort builds the mental toughness needed to handle bigger challenges when they arise.

Develop a Growth Mindset[1]. A growth mindset is a belief that your abilities and intelligence can be developed through effort and learning (Dweck, 2006). Instead of seeing failures as proof of inadequacy, view them as growth opportunities. This mindset shift is crucial for building resilience because it allows you to see challenges as a normal part of the learning process rather than as insurmountable obstacles.

Practice Gratitude. It might seem counterintuitive, but practicing gratitude can build mental toughness. Focusing on what you're grateful for shifts your perspective away from what's going wrong to what's going right. This positive outlook makes it easier to handle adversity because you're more likely to see the silver lining in difficult situations (Emmons & McCullough, 2003).

---

[1] Growth mindset refers to the belief that abilities and intelligence can be developed through effort, learning, and persistence. This concept contrasts with a fixed mindset, which assumes that abilities are static and unchangeable.

Visualize Success. Mental imagery is a powerful tool for building resilience. Spend a few minutes each day visualizing yourself overcoming challenges and succeeding in your goals. This practice boosts confidence and prepares your mind to handle adversity by creating a mental blueprint for success (Taylor et al., 1998).

Set Small, Achievable Goals. Start by setting small, achievable goals that build up to larger ones. Each time you accomplish a goal, it builds confidence and resilience. Over time, these small victories accumulate, giving you the mental toughness to take on bigger challenges.

Managing Stress and Avoiding Burnout

Stress is inevitable, but how you manage it determines whether it becomes a source of strength or leads to burnout. Here are some techniques to help you manage stress and avoid burnout.

Prioritize Self-Care. Self-care isn't a luxury; it's a necessity. Regular exercise, a balanced diet, and sufficient sleep are foundational to managing stress. When your body is well-nourished and rested, your mind is better equipped to handle stress (Shields et al., 2017).

Practice Mindful Breathing. Mindful breathing exercises can help you manage acute stress by activating the body's relaxation response. Try deep breathing techniques, such as inhaling for a count of four, holding for four, and exhaling for four. This simple practice can reduce stress hormones and calm your mind, making it easier to stay focused under pressure (Brown & Gerbarg, 2005).

Set Boundaries. One of the leading causes of burnout is taking on too much. Learn to set clear boundaries around your time and energy. This might mean saying no to additional responsibilities, limiting your work hours, or setting aside time each day for relaxation and hobbies.

Take Regular Breaks. The human brain isn't designed to focus for hours on end without a break. Implement techniques like the

Pomodoro Technique, where you work for 25 minutes and then take a 5-minute break. Regular breaks prevent mental fatigue and help you maintain high levels of focus and productivity (Cirillo, 2006).

Engage in Regular Reflection. Take time each week to reflect on what's working in your life and what isn't. This practice helps you identify stressors early and make adjustments before they lead to burnout. Regular reflection also reinforces your sense of purpose, reminding you why you're working toward your goals in the first place.

Resilience Supports a Life Focused

Resilience is the backbone of a focused life. It's what allows you to keep going when the going gets tough and to maintain your focus on what truly matters, even in the face of adversity. Here's how resilience supports your ability to stay focused.

Managing Clarity During Challenges. When resilient, you're less likely to be overwhelmed by challenges. Instead of getting lost in the chaos, you maintain clarity about your goals and priorities. This clarity lets you make decisions that keep you on track, even when life gets complicated.

Bouncing Back from Setbacks. Everyone faces setbacks, but resilient people bounce back faster. They don't dwell on failures or let them derail their progress. Instead, they learn from their mistakes and use those lessons to come back stronger. This ability to recover quickly ensures that setbacks don't become permanent roadblocks (Tugade & Fredrickson, 2004).

Sustaining Long-Term Focus. Achieving big goals requires sustained effort over time, and resilience is crucial in maintaining that effort. It keeps you motivated and committed, even when the initial excitement wears off or when progress seems slow. Resilience makes you more likely to stay the course and achieve long-term success.

Protecting Your Well-Being. Resilience isn't just about achieving goals; it's also about protecting your well-being. By managing stress effectively and avoiding burnout, resilience helps you stay healthy and energized so you have the stamina to pursue what truly matters over the long haul.

Building mental resilience takes time and effort, but it's a skill that will serve you well in every aspect of your life. With resilience, you're better equipped to handle challenges, maintain focus, and keep moving toward your goals—no matter the obstacles.

Staying Grounded in Your Purpose

No matter how strong your focus is or how resilient your mindset is, life will inevitably throw challenges your way. When it does, staying grounded in your purpose will keep you on track. This section will provide practical strategies to ensure that your core values and priorities remain at the forefront, even when life gets chaotic.

Staying Connected to Your Core Values and Priorities

Staying connected to your core values and priorities requires consistent effort. Here are some daily practices to help you maintain that connection.

Morning Rituals. Start each day with a routine that reinforces your core values and priorities. This might include reading a passage from a book that inspires you, writing in a journal, or setting intentions for the day. By beginning your day with purpose, you set the tone for everything that follows.

Example. If personal growth is one of your core values, dedicate 15 minutes each morning to reading a book, taking an online course, or reflecting on what you learned the previous day.

Daily Reflection. At the end of each day, take a few minutes to reflect on how your actions aligned with your values and priorities. Ask yourself. Did I focus on what truly matters today? What could

I have done differently? This simple practice helps you stay connected to your purpose and identifies areas for improvement.

> ***Example.*** Keep a journal where you jot down your reflections each evening. Over time, this record will help you see patterns in your behavior and make adjustments as needed.

Mindful Check-Ins. Pause to check in with yourself throughout the day. Are you staying true to your priorities, or have you drifted into distraction? These brief moments of mindfulness help you course-correct in real-time, ensuring that your actions align with your purpose.

> ***Example.*** Set reminders on your phone to take a few deep breaths and check in with your intentions. This practice can be beneficial during busy or stressful times.

Gratitude Practice. Practicing gratitude is a powerful way to stay grounded in what matters most. By regularly acknowledging the things you're thankful for, you reinforce your connection to your values and the positive aspects of your life.

> ***Example.*** Write down three things you're grateful for each morning or evening. Focus on how these elements reflect your core values and contribute to your overall sense of purpose.

Reflection and Self-Assessment in Maintaining Focus

Reflection and self-assessment are crucial for maintaining focus and ensuring that you're living in alignment with your purpose. Without regular reflection, it's easy to lose sight of your goals and get caught up in the daily grind. Here's why reflection and self-assessment matter.

> **Clarity and Direction.** Reflection helps you gain clarity about where you're headed and whether your current actions are taking you there. It's an opportunity to assess your progress, identify misalignments, and make necessary adjustments.

> > ***Practical Tip.*** Schedule a weekly review where you assess your goals, progress, and any challenges you face. Use this time to realign your actions with your core values.

Continuous Improvement. Self-assessment fosters a mindset of continuous improvement. By regularly evaluating your actions and decisions, you can learn from your experiences and make better choices in the future. This ongoing process helps you stay focused on your long-term goals.

Practical Tip. Conduct a brief self-assessment after each significant project or task. What went well? What could have been better? How can you apply these lessons moving forward?

Staying True to Your Purpose. Reflection helps you stay connected to your purpose, even during challenging times. When life gets chaotic, it's easy to get swept away by external pressures. Regular reflection grounds you in your values and priorities, providing a stable foundation to navigate difficulties.

Practical Tip. Use reflective journaling to explore your thoughts and feelings about your purpose. Write about why your core values matter to you and how they guide your actions.

How to Stay Grounded in Your Purpose

Chaos is inevitable, but it doesn't have to derail you from your purpose. Here's how to stay grounded when life gets overwhelming.

Simplify Your Focus. When life gets hectic, simplify your focus. Identify the one or two priorities that are most important to you right now and concentrate your efforts on those. By narrowing your focus, you reduce things that overwhelm and ensure that your most critical values remain intact.

Example. If your work and family life are both demanding attention, focus on maintaining quality time with your loved ones while meeting your most essential work obligations. Let go of less important tasks until the chaos subsides.

Practice Acceptance. Accept that you can't control everything. Life is unpredictable, and sometimes things won't go according to plan. Instead of resisting or getting frustrated, practice acceptance.

Recognize that chaos is temporary, and focus on what you can control—your actions and responses.

Example. When faced with an unexpected challenge, take a deep breath and remind yourself that this, too, shall pass. Ask yourself. What's the most constructive action I can take right now?

Lean on Your Support System. Staying grounded in your purpose doesn't mean going it alone. During chaotic times, lean on your support system—friends, family, and mentors. They can offer perspective, encouragement, and practical help to keep you on track.

Example. Reach out to a trusted friend or mentor when overwhelmed. Share your challenges and ask for advice or simply a listening ear.

Return to Your Rituals. When life gets chaotic, it's easy to abandon the routines and rituals that keep you grounded. Instead, make a conscious effort to maintain these practices. They provide stability and a sense of normalcy, helping you stay connected to your purpose.

Example. Even when your schedule is packed, find time for your morning meditation or evening journaling. These small acts can significantly impact your mental and emotional well-being.

Reaffirm Your Purpose. Amid the chaos, take a moment to reaffirm your purpose. Remind yourself why you do what you do and how your actions align with your core values. This simple act can re-center you and renew your commitment to staying focused.

Example. Create a personal mission statement or mantra that encapsulates your purpose. Repeat it to yourself when you're feeling lost or overwhelmed.

Staying grounded in your purpose requires intentionality and practice, especially when life gets chaotic. By implementing these strategies, you can maintain a solid connection to your values and priorities, ensuring that you continue to move forward with focus and purpose, no matter the challenges.

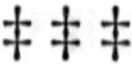

3

Applications in Key Areas of Life

Relationships: Quality over Quantity

If you want your relationships to be significant, it's not about having a lot of connections—it's about having the right ones. Building and maintaining relationships that align with your values will enrich your life and keep you focused on what truly matters.

Build and Maintain Meaningful Relationships That Align with Your Values

The first step in building meaningful relationships is understanding your core values. When you know what matters most, you can seek out and nurture relationships with people who share similar values. These connections will be more fulfilling and sustainable because they're based on mutual understanding and respect (Rokeach, 1973).

Here's how to ensure your relationships align with your values.

Clarify Your Values. Start by identifying the values that are most important to you—whether it's honesty, loyalty, growth, or kindness. Once you're clear on your values, look for those qualities in others. Surround yourself with people who reflect and respect these values (Schwartz, 2012).

Example. If personal growth is a core value, build relationships with individuals committed to continuous learning and self-improvement.

Be Selective. You don't need to be friends with everyone. Being selective about who you let into your inner circle is okay. Focus on quality over quantity—cultivate a few deep, meaningful relationships rather than trying to maintain superficial connections with many people (Dunbar, 1992).

Practical Tip. When meeting new people, ask whether their values align with yours. If not, consider whether it's worth building a relationship.

Invest in Relationships. Building meaningful relationships requires time and effort. Make it a priority to invest in the relationships that matter most to you. This might mean regularly checking in with a close friend, planning quality time with your partner, or offering support to a family member (Reis & Shaver, 1988).

Example. Schedule regular catch-ups with your closest friends, even just a quick phone call. Consistency is critical to maintaining strong connections.

Communicate Openly. Open and honest communication is the foundation of any meaningful relationship. Be clear about your values and expectations, and encourage others to do the same. This transparency helps build trust and ensures that your relationships remain aligned with what matters most to you (Gottman & Silver, 1999).

Practical Tip. Practice active listening—give your full attention when someone is speaking, and respond thoughtfully. This shows respect and strengthens your connection.

Fostering Deep Connections

Deep connections don't happen by accident—they require intentional effort. Here are some strategies to help you foster meaningful connections with the important people in your life.

Prioritize Quality Time. Spending quality time together is essential for building deep connections. Whether with your partner, family, or friends, ensure you're engaging in activities that allow for meaningful interaction (Csikszentmihalyi, 1990).

Example. Instead of just watching TV with your partner, plan activities that encourage conversation, like cooking together or walking.

Be Present. In today's digital world, it's easy to be physically present but mentally checked out. Make a conscious effort to be fully present when you're with others. Put away your phone, make eye contact, and engage in the moment (Turkle, 2015).

Practical Tip. Establish "tech-free" times during meals or family gatherings to encourage real interaction.

Show Appreciation. Regularly expressing gratitude and appreciation is a powerful way to deepen connections. Let the people in your life know how much they mean to you and why you value your relationship with them (Emmons & McCullough, 2003).

Example. Write a heartfelt note to a friend or partner, acknowledging their positive impact on your life.

Support Each Other's Growth. True connections are built on mutual support. Encourage the people in your life to pursue their goals and passions, and be there to celebrate their successes and help them through challenges (Deci & Ryan, 2000).

Practical Tip. Set goals with your partner or a close friend, and hold each other accountable. This shared journey can strengthen your bond.

Managing Relationships That Drain Energy or Distract from Your Goals

Not all relationships are positive; some can drain your energy or distract you from your goals. It's important to recognize these relationships and take steps to manage them effectively.

Identify Energy Drainers. Reflect on how you feel after interacting with certain people. Do they leave you feeling energized and uplifted or drained and stressed? Be honest about which relationships negatively impact your well-being (Goleman, 1995).

Example. If you consistently feel exhausted after spending time with a particular friend, it might be time to reassess the relationship.

Set Boundaries. Setting clear boundaries is crucial when dealing with relationships that drain your energy. This might mean limiting your time with certain people or being clear about what you're willing and unwilling to tolerate (Cloud & Townsend, 1992).

Practical Tip. When setting boundaries, use "I" statements such as "I need some time to recharge, so I won't be able to meet up this week."

Reevaluate and Adjust. Sometimes, relationships evolve, and what once aligned with your values no longer does. It's okay to step back or let go of relationships that no longer serve you. Reevaluate your connections regularly and adjust as needed to stay focused on your goals (Pronk & Righart, 2016).

Example. If a friendship has become toxic or one-sided, consider having an honest conversation about how you feel. If things don't improve, it may be time to distance yourself.

Focus on Positive Relationships. Invest more time and energy in the positive ones to counterbalance any draining relationships. Surround yourself with people who inspire, support, and uplift you. These relationships will help you focus on what truly matters (Lyubomirsky et al., 2005).

Practical Tip. List the people who bring out the best in you and prioritize spending time with them.

Building and maintaining meaningful relationships that align with your values is critical to living a focused and fulfilling life. By prioritizing quality over quantity, fostering deep connections, and managing relationships that drain your energy, you'll create a supportive network that helps you stay true to your purpose and achieve your goals.

Career: Aligning Work with Your Values

If your career isn't aligned with your values, you'll constantly feel disconnected between what you do and what truly matters to you. Aligning your work with your core values isn't just about job satisfaction—it's about leading a fulfilling and purposeful life. Here's how to ensure your career reflects what truly matters to you.

Ensuring Your Career Reflects What Truly Matters to You

To align your career with your values, you must first understand them and then make deliberate choices that align your work with them. Here's how to do it.

Identify Your Core Values. Clarify your core values before making career decisions. These principles guide your decisions and give meaning to your life. Typical values might include creativity, helping others, autonomy, or financial security (Schwartz, 2012). Once you've identified your values, evaluate your current job to see how well it aligns with them.

Example. If autonomy is a core value, but your current job involves micromanagement, you may need to seek a more independent role.

Assess Your Current Role. Take a hard look at your current position. Does it allow you to live out your values or force you to compromise them? Identify areas of alignment and misalignment. This will help you determine whether you need to adjust your approach to your current role or consider a different path altogether (Wrzesniewski et al., 1997).

Practical Tip. List your job responsibilities and match them against your values. When there's a mismatch, brainstorm ways to shift your approach or initiate a discussion with your supervisor to make changes.

Seek Alignment Through Job Crafting. Job crafting involves reshaping your role to fit your values and strengths better. This could mean taking on projects that align with your interests, seeking out tasks that match your skills, or changing how you think about your work to find more meaning in what you do (Berg et al., 2013).

Example. If helping others is a crucial value, look for opportunities within your current job to mentor colleagues, lead a community outreach program, or work on projects that benefit others.

Make Strategic Career Moves. If your current job doesn't align with your values and can't be adjusted, it might be time to consider a change. Look for roles or companies that share your values. Research potential employers thoroughly—look at their mission statements, workplace culture, and the experiences of current employees (Schein, 2010).

Practical Tip. Network with professionals in fields or companies that interest you. Learn about their experiences to see if those roles align better with your values.

Align Daily Tasks with Values. Even in a less-than-ideal job, you can often find ways to align daily tasks with your values. This might involve approaching tasks with a different mindset, focusing on aspects of your work that align with your values, or finding small ways to incorporate what matters to you into your daily routine (Hackman & Oldham, 1976).

Example. If creativity is important to you, find ways to bring creativity into routine tasks, such as proposing new solutions to problems or improving existing processes.

Purposeful Work and How to Find or Create It

Purposeful work is work that feels meaningful and is aligned with your values and passions. It's not just about what you do but why you do it. Here's why purposeful work matters and how to find or create it.

Purpose Drives Motivation. When your work is purposeful, you're more motivated, engaged, and satisfied. Purpose gives you a reason to get up in the morning and face the day's challenges. It's the difference between working to pay the bills and working because you believe in your actions (Pink, 2009).

Identify What Gives You Purpose. Reflect on what aspects of your work or past experiences have felt most meaningful to you. What projects have you been most proud of? What activities make you lose track of time? These are clues to what gives you purpose (Csikszentmihalyi, 1990).

Practical Tip. Write down three to five moments when you felt fulfilled in your career. Look for patterns or common themes—these will point you toward what makes work meaningful.

Create Purpose in Your Current Role. You don't always need to change jobs to find purpose. Sometimes, it's about changing your approach to your current role. Look for ways to connect your daily tasks to a larger purpose, whether helping others, contributing to a bigger mission, or improving your community (Berg et al., 2013).

Example. If your job involves data analysis, consider how your work helps the company make better decisions, benefiting employees and customers.

Find or Create a Role with Purpose. If your current job is a poor fit for your values and you can't find purpose, it may be time to seek a new role. Look for positions that align with your values, or consider creating your path through entrepreneurship, freelancing, or consulting (Schein, 2010).

Practical Tip. When considering new opportunities, ask potential employers about their values and how they see your role contributing to the company's mission.

Balancing Career Ambitions with Other Life Priorities

Balancing your career with other life priorities is essential for maintaining overall well-being. Here's how to ensure that your career ambitions don't overshadow other important aspects of your life.

Set Clear Boundaries. Establish boundaries between work and personal life. This might involve setting specific work hours, creating a dedicated workspace at home, or turning off work-related notifications after a specific time. Clear boundaries help you stay focused during work hours and fully present during personal time (Derks et al., 2014).

Practical Tip. Communicate your boundaries to colleagues and supervisors. For example, let them know when you won't be available outside of work hours.

Prioritize What Matters Most. Identify your top life priorities—family, health, personal growth, or hobbies—and make sure your career supports them rather than detracts from them. This might mean adjusting your career ambitions to align with your broader life goals (Greenhaus & Powell, 2006).

Example. If family time is a priority, consider roles that offer flexibility or remote work options.

Practice Time Management. Effective time management balances career ambitions with other priorities. Use tools like time blocking, to-do lists, and calendar management to ensure you make time for all aspects of your life (Covey, 1989).

Practical Tip. Schedule time for personal activities as you would for work tasks. This ensures that your priorities get the attention they deserve.

Regularly Reevaluate Your Priorities. Life changes, and so do your priorities. Regularly assess whether your career still aligns with your values and life goals. If not, adjust to bring things back into balance (Super, 1990).

Practical Tip. Set aside time every few months to reflect on your career and personal life. Ask yourself whether you spend time on what matters and make changes as needed.

By aligning your career with your values, seeking purposeful work, and balancing your job with other life priorities, you'll create a professional life that supports your financial goals and enriches your overall sense of fulfillment and purpose.

Personal Growth. Continuous Improvement with a Purpose

Personal growth should be more than just ticking off boxes or jumping on the latest self-help trend. It should be a deliberate, focused effort to improve in areas that truly matter to you. If your development efforts don't align with your core values, they can quickly become distractions rather than pathways to meaningful improvement.

Focus Your Personal Development Efforts on Areas That Align with Your Values

The key to effective personal growth is ensuring your efforts align with your core values. Here's how to make sure your self-improvement journey is purposeful.

Clarify Your Values. Start by identifying your core values, which are the compass for your personal growth. Ask yourself what's most important—integrity, creativity, family, or health. Once you're clear on your values, you can focus on areas that reflect and support these principles (Schwartz, 2012).

> ***Example.*** If health is a core value, prioritize personal development activities that enhance your physical and mental well-being, such as regular exercise, meditation, or learning about nutrition.

Set Specific, Values-Based Goals. Align your personal development goals with your core values. Vague goals like "become a better person" are hard to measure and may not lead to meaningful change. Instead, set specific, actionable goals that directly relate to your values (Locke & Latham, 2002).

> ***Practical Tip.*** Instead of setting a general goal like "improve my skills," choose something more focused, such as "learn a new language to enhance my communication abilities," especially if communication is a crucial value for you.

Prioritize Quality Over Quantity. It's easy to get caught up in doing too much at once—reading every self-help book, taking numerous courses, or adopting multiple new habits. However, focusing on a few deeply aligned areas with your values is more effective than spreading yourself too thin (Covey, 1989).

> ***Practical Tip.*** Focus on one or two areas at a time. This allows you to dedicate time and energy to growing in those areas.

Regularly Reflect and Adjust. Personal growth isn't a one-time effort—it's a continuous process. Regularly reflect on your progress and assess whether your efforts align with your values. If not, adjust your goals and strategies accordingly (Schon, 1983).

> ***Practical Tip.*** Schedule a monthly check-in with yourself to review your goals, celebrate progress, and make any necessary adjustments to stay on track with your values.

Lifelong Learning in Living a Focused Life

Lifelong learning isn't just about acquiring new knowledge—it's about staying curious and adaptable in a constantly changing world. Here's why lifelong learning is essential for a focused life.

Keeps You Adaptable. The world and the challenges and opportunities you'll face constantly evolve. Lifelong learning helps you stay adaptable and open to new ideas, which is crucial for maintaining focus in a dynamic environment (Senge, 1990).

> ***Practical Tip.*** Make it a habit to learn something new regularly—through books, online courses, or even conversations with others. This keeps your mind sharp and ready to adapt to change.

Enhances Your Ability to Align with Your Values. Continuous learning allows you to deepen your understanding of the areas that most matter to you. Whether learning new skills that align with your career values or exploring new perspectives that enhance your personal growth, lifelong learning strengthens your ability to live in alignment with your values (Kolb, 1984).

> ***Example.*** If sustainability is a core value, commit to learning about environmental practices, sustainable living, or renewable energy technologies.

Fosters a Growth Mindset. Embracing lifelong learning cultivates a growth mindset—believing that your abilities and intelligence can be developed through effort and learning (Dweck, 2006). This mindset is crucial for staying motivated and focused on personal growth, even when faced with challenges.

Practical Tip. Approach setbacks as learning opportunities. Reflect on what went wrong, what you can learn from the experience, and how to improve.

Builds Resilience and Confidence. As you learn and grow, you build confidence in your ability to handle new situations and challenges. This resilience is critical to maintaining focus and staying grounded in your purpose, especially when life gets tough (Tough, 2012).

Practical Tip. Take on challenges that stretch your abilities. Each time you push beyond your comfort zone, you build resilience and confidence to serve you in all areas of life.

The Trap of Self-Improvement

Not all self-improvement efforts are created equal. It's easy to fall into the trap of pursuing personal growth for the sake of it rather than because it aligns with your values. Here's how to avoid that pitfall.

Beware of the "Productivity Trap". In a world that glorifies busyness and productivity, it's easy to equate constant self-improvement with progress. However, being busy doesn't necessarily mean you're growing in meaningful ways. Focus on purposeful growth that aligns with your values rather than simply trying to do more (Newport, 2016).

Practical Tip. Before taking on a new self-improvement project, ask yourself, "How does this align with my values? What specific benefit will it bring to my life?"

Avoid Comparison. With the rise of social media, it's easy to compare your growth journey with others. However, everyone's values and goals differ, so what's suitable for someone else may not be right for you. Focus on your path and progress (Festinger, 1954).

> ***Practical Tip.*** Limit your exposure to social media or environments where you compare your growth to others. Instead, focus on your personal goals and the progress you're making.

Don't Chase Trends. Just because it's a popular self-improvement trend doesn't mean it's right for you. Whether it's the latest diet, productivity hack, or meditation technique, ensure it aligns with your values before diving in (Clear, 2018).

> ***Practical Tip.*** Before adopting a new trend, do your research. Consider whether it genuinely aligns with your goals and values or if it's just the flavor of the month.

Regularly Reevaluate Your Efforts. Personal growth should be a deliberate and purposeful journey. Regularly reevaluate your efforts to ensure they still serve you and align with your values. If they're not, changing course is okay (Schon, 1983).

> ***Practical Tip.*** Review your development efforts at the end of each quarter. Identify what's working and not, and make adjustments as needed.

By focusing your growth efforts on areas that align with your values, embracing lifelong learning, and avoiding the trap of self-improvement for its own sake, you'll ensure that your journey of continuous improvement is purposeful and meaningful. This approach will help you focus on what matters, leading to a more fulfilling and balanced life.

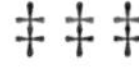

4

The Discipline of Daily Focus

*"Success is the sum of small efforts,
repeated day in and day out."*

— *Robert Collier*

Creating Routines that Reflect Your Priorities

If you want to live a life focused on what truly matters, your daily routines must reflect your priorities. Designing routines that support your core values is essential for maintaining focus and achieving your goals.

Design Daily Routines that Support What Matters Most

Your daily routine is more than just a series of tasks—it's the foundation upon which your entire life is built. To ensure that your routine supports your priorities, you must be intentional about how you structure your day.

Identify Your Priorities. The first step is clearly identifying what matters most to you. These might include your career, family, health, personal growth, or spiritual practice. Once you've identified your top priorities, you can design routines that support them (Covey, 1989).

> ***Example.*** If health is a priority, your routine should include time for exercise, meal planning, and sleep. If personal growth is important, allocate reading, learning, or skill development time.

Align Your Routines with Your Energy Levels. Not all hours of the day are created equal. Some people are most productive in the morning, while others hit their stride in the afternoon or evening. Align your most important tasks with the times when you have the most energy and focus (Duhigg, 2012).

> ***Practical Tip.*** If you're a morning person, schedule your most challenging or creative tasks for the first few hours of the day. Reserve less demanding tasks for times when your energy dips.

Start with a Morning Routine. A strong morning routine sets the tone for the rest of the day. It doesn't have to be complicated, but it should include activities that align with your values and priorities. This might include exercise, meditation, journaling, or planning your day (Hal Elrod, 2012).

> ***Example.*** A simple morning routine could include 10 minutes of stretching, 15 minutes of meditation, and 20 minutes of reading or journaling. These activities can help you start the day with clarity and intention.

Use Time Blocking. Time blocking is a technique where you schedule specific blocks of time for different activities throughout your day. This ensures that your most important tasks get the attention they deserve rather than getting lost in the shuffle of less important activities (Newport, 2016).

Practical Tip. Use a calendar to block out time for each of your priorities. For example, set aside time in the morning for deep work, mid-day for meetings, and late afternoon for exercise.

Incorporate Reflection Time. Regular reflection ensures that your routines align with your priorities. Set aside time each day or week to reflect on what's working, what isn't, and how you can make adjustments (Schon, 1983).

Practical Tip. Spend 10 minutes each evening reviewing your day. Ask yourself whether your activities are aligned with your values and priorities, and make adjustments as needed.

Consistency and Discipline in Maintaining Focus

Consistency and discipline are the backbone of any successful routine. Without them, even the best-laid plans can fall apart. Here's why they matter.

Builds Momentum. Consistent actions, even small ones, build momentum over time. When you stick to your routines, you create positive habits that make it easier to stay focused on your priorities (Clear, 2018).

Example. If you consistently exercise every morning, it becomes a habit that requires less mental effort and willpower over time.

Reduces Decision Fatigue. When your routines are consistent, you reduce the number of decisions you must make daily. This frees up mental energy for more important tasks, helping you maintain focus throughout the day (Baumeister & Tierney, 2011).

Practical Tip. Automate routine decisions—such as what to wear, eat, or do first thing in the morning—so you can save your mental energy for more meaningful choices.

Creates Stability. Discipline and consistency create a sense of stability in your life, which is especially important during times of stress or change. When your routines are solid, they provide a reliable foundation that helps you stay grounded and focused (Dweck, 2006).

Example. Sticking to your morning routine can provide a sense of normalcy and control even during busy or challenging times.

Routines and Habits of Highly Focused Individuals

Let's examine some examples of routines and habits from highly focused individuals. These examples can inspire you as you design your routines.

Morning Routine of Benjamin Franklin. Franklin famously structured his day with a consistent morning routine that included asking himself, "What good shall I do this day?" He would plan his day, review his goals, and reflect personally (Franklin, 1791).

Takeaway. Start your day with intention by setting goals and reflecting on how to make a positive impact.

Time-Blocking Technique of Elon Musk. Elon Musk is known for his rigorous time-blocking schedule, dividing his day into five-minute increments. This allows him to maximize productivity and ensure his time is spent on high-priority tasks (Vance, 2015).

Takeaway. Use time blocking to ensure that your most important tasks get the necessary time and attention.

Focused Work Sessions of Cal Newport. Cal Newport, author of *Deep Work*, advocates for dedicated, distraction-free work sessions. He schedules specific blocks of time for deep work, focusing solely on cognitively demanding tasks (Newport, 2016).

Takeaway. Dedicate specific blocks of time each day to focus on your most important work without interruptions.

By designing routines that reflect your priorities, maintaining consistency and discipline, and learning from the habits of highly focused individuals, you can create a daily structure that keeps you aligned with what truly matters. This approach will help you stay focused, productive, and fulfilled in all areas of your life.

Time Management for a Purposeful Life

If you're serious about living a purposeful life, you need to get a handle on your time. Time management isn't just about getting more done—it's about ensuring you spend your time on what truly matters. Here's how to manage your time effectively to stay focused on your priorities.

Managing Your Time Effectively to Focus on Your Priorities

Time is your most valuable resource, and how you manage it directly impacts your ability to achieve your goals. Here are some proven techniques to help you use your time wisely.

Prioritize Your Tasks. Not all tasks are created equal. Focus on the tasks that impact your goals and values most. The Pareto Principle, also known as the 80/20 rule, suggests that 80% of your results come from 20% of your efforts (Koch, 1998). Identify the tasks that fall into that crucial 20% and make them your top priority.

Example. If your goal is to advance in your career, prioritize tasks that contribute directly to your professional growth, such as completing important projects, networking, or learning new skills.

Batch Similar Tasks Together. Batching involves grouping similar tasks and tackling them in one go rather than switching between different tasks throughout the day. This reduces the mental energy lost in task-switching and helps you maintain focus (Newport, 2016).

Practical Tip. Set aside specific times during the day to handle emails, make phone calls, or complete administrative tasks. This allows you to focus on deep work without constant interruptions.

Set Clear Boundaries. To protect your time, you must set clear boundaries with others. This might mean saying no to unnecessary meetings, limiting social media use, or setting specific times when you're available for interruptions (Baumeister & Tierney, 2011).

Practical Tip. Communicate your boundaries to colleagues and family members. For example, let them know when you're in a focused work session and not to be disturbed unless it's urgent.

Use the Pomodoro Technique. The Pomodoro Technique involves working in focused intervals, typically 25 minutes, followed by a short break. This method helps maintain focus and prevent burnout by breaking your work into manageable chunks (Cirillo, 2006).

Practical Tip. Set a timer for 25 minutes and work on a single task. After the timer goes off, take a 5-minute break before starting the next session. Repeat this cycle to stay productive and focused.

Review and Reflect Regularly. Regularly reviewing your time management practices allows you to make adjustments and ensure your time is spent on what truly matters. Set aside time each week to reflect on your productivity and identify areas for improvement (Covey, 1989).

Practical Tip. Spend 10-15 minutes at the end of each week reviewing your tasks and how well they aligned with your priorities. Use this reflection to plan for the week ahead.

Scheduling, Delegation, and Time Blocking in Maintaining Focus

Effective time management isn't just about working harder; it's about working smarter. Scheduling, delegation, and time blocking are key strategies that help you stay focused and productive.

Scheduling. A well-structured schedule is essential for managing your time effectively. Planning your day in advance allows you to allocate time to your most important tasks and ensure that nothing slips through the cracks. A good schedule also helps you balance work with personal time, reducing the risk of burnout (Gawande, 2010).

Practical Tip. At the end of each day, plan your schedule for the next day. Prioritize tasks based on urgency and importance and include breaks to recharge.

Delegation. You don't have to do everything yourself. Delegating tasks to others allows you to focus on the activities that only you can do—those that align most closely with your values and priorities (Covey, 1989). Effective delegation requires clear communication and trust in the abilities of those you're delegating to.

Practical Tip. Identify tasks that can be delegated to others, whether at work or home. Provide clear instructions and set expectations to ensure the task meets your standards.

Time Blocking. Time blocking involves dividing your day into blocks dedicated to a specific task or activity. This approach helps you focus on one thing at a time and prevents multitasking, which can dilute your efforts and reduce productivity (Newport, 2016).

Practical Tip. Use your calendar to block out time for different activities. For example, you might block out 9. 00 AM to 11. 00 AM for deep work, 1. 00 PM to 2. 00 PM for meetings, and 3. 00 PM to 4. 00 PM for personal development.

Avoiding Common Time-Wasters and Distractions

In today's fast-paced world, distractions are everywhere. Here's how to avoid common time-wasters and stay focused on your priorities.

Limit Social Media Use. Social media can be a major time-waster if not appropriately managed. Set specific times during the day to check your accounts and avoid mindless scrolling that wastes valuable time (Newport, 2019).

> ***Practical Tip.*** Use apps or browser extensions that limit your social media time. For example, you can set a 15-minute daily limit on your favorite social media sites.

Turn Off Notifications. Constant emails, messages, and app notifications can distract your attention from important tasks. Turn off non-essential notifications to minimize distractions and maintain focus (Rosen et al., 2013).

> ***Practical Tip.*** Set your phone to "Do Not Disturb" mode during focused work sessions, and check notifications only during scheduled breaks.

Avoid Multitasking. Multitasking may seem like a way to get more done, but it often leads to reduced productivity and lower-quality work. Focus on one task at a time to ensure you give it your full attention (González & Mark, 2004).

> ***Practical Tip.*** Use time blocking to dedicate specific times for each task, and resist the urge to switch between tasks before one is completed.

Beware of Procrastination. Procrastination is a common time-waster that can derail productivity. Combat it by breaking tasks into smaller, manageable steps and tackling them simultaneously (Steel, 2007).

> ***Practical Tip.*** Start with the smallest possible step on a task you avoid. Often, just getting started is enough to build momentum.

By implementing these time management techniques—prioritizing tasks, scheduling effectively, delegating when possible, and avoiding common distractions—you'll be better equipped to focus on what truly matters. This disciplined approach to time management will help you live a more purposeful and fulfilling life.

Maintaining Focus in a Distracting World

In today's world, distractions are everywhere, and staying focused is harder than ever. Whether it's the constant ping of notifications, the allure of social media, or the noise of everyday life, external distractions can easily pull you away from what truly matters. Here's how to maintain focus and create an environment that supports your goals.

Strategies for Dealing with External Distractions Like Technology, Social Media, and Noise

To maintain focus in a world filled with distractions, you need a strategic approach to managing the external factors that vie for your attention. Here are some effective strategies.

Limit Your Exposure to Technology and Social Media. Technology and social media are among the biggest distractions in modern life. They can easily consume hours of your day if not appropriately managed. Set clear boundaries for how and when you use these tools (Newport, 2019).

Practical Tip. Designate specific times during the day to check emails, social media, and messages. Outside of these times, keep your phone and other devices out of sight to reduce temptation.

Use Tools to Block Distractions. Numerous apps and tools are designed to help you stay focused by blocking distracting websites and apps. Tools like *Freedom, Cold Turkey,* and *Focus@Will* can help you stay on task by limiting your access to distractions during work sessions (Rosen et al., 2013).

Practical Tip. Install a website blocker on your computer and set it to block distracting sites during your most productive hours.

Manage Noise and Create a Quiet Environment. Noise can be distracting, especially in open or busy environments. Use noise-canceling headphones, white noise machines, or calming music to create a more focused work environment (Banbury & Berry, 2005).

Practical Tip. If you work in a noisy environment, use noise-canceling headphones or listen to instrumental music that helps you concentrate.

Practice Mindfulness and Focused Breathing. When distractions arise, practicing mindfulness can help you stay centered and return to the task. Focused breathing exercises can also reduce stress and improve concentration (Kabat-Zinn, 1994).

Practical Tip. When you feel distracted, take a few deep breaths and return your attention to your breath. This simple exercise can help refocus your mind.

Create Digital Boundaries. Digital distractions can be particularly challenging because they're always within reach. Set boundaries around using digital devices, such as turning off notifications during work hours or leaving your phone in another room while you work (Turkle, 2015).

Practical Tip. Use "Do Not Disturb" mode to silence notifications during focused work periods.

Create a Focused Environment at Home and Work

Your environment plays a crucial role in your ability to maintain focus. You can create an atmosphere that supports deep work and productivity by intentionally designing your home and workspaces to minimize distractions.

Declutter Your Space. A cluttered space can lead to a cluttered mind. Keep your workspace tidy and free from unnecessary items that might distract you. A clean and organized environment promotes clarity and focus (Vohs et al., 2013).

Practical Tip. Spend a few minutes each day tidying your workspace. Keep only essential items on your desk and store everything else out of sight.

Designate a Dedicated Workspace. Having a specific place for work can help you mentally separate work time from personal time, making it easier to focus when you're in that space. Ideally, this space should be quiet, comfortable, and free from distractions (Gawande, 2010).

Practical Tip. Set up a home office or a designated corner of a room solely for work. Use this space only for work-related activities to reinforce the mental boundary.

Control Your Environment's Sensory Input. Your senses can enhance or hinder your focus. Consider the lighting, temperature, and scent of your workspace. Natural light, a comfortable temperature, and calming scents like lavender can create a more focused environment (Edwards & Torcellini, 2002).

Practical Tip. Open curtains to let in natural light, adjust the temperature to your comfort, and use a diffuser with essential oils like lavender or eucalyptus to create a calming atmosphere.

Incorporate Focus Cues. Small environmental cues can help you maintain focus. This could be a particular piece of music, a specific chair you sit in for work, or a visual reminder of your goals. These cues signal your brain that it's time to focus (Duhigg, 2012).

Practical Tip. Choose a specific playlist or background noise you use only during focused work sessions. Over time, your brain will associate this sound with deep focus.

The Importance of Digital Detoxes and Periodic Disconnection

In our hyper-connected world, taking regular breaks from digital devices is essential for maintaining focus and mental clarity. Here's why digital detoxes and periodic disconnection are crucial.

Reduces Cognitive Overload. Constant exposure to digital information can lead to cognitive overload, making it difficult to focus and process information effectively. A digital detox allows your brain to rest and reset (Small & Vorgan, 2008).

Practical Tip. Schedule regular digital detoxes, such as a few hours each evening without screens or a full day each weekend dedicated to offline activities.

Improves Mental Well-Being. Studies have shown that excessive screen time is linked to increased stress, anxiety, and depression. Disconnecting from digital devices can help reduce these adverse effects and improve overall well-being (Twenge, 2017).

Practical Tip. Incorporate daily periods of disconnection, such as during meals or before bed, to improve your mental health and focus.

Enhances Real-Life Connections. Digital detoxes allow you to connect more deeply with the people around you. By stepping away from screens, you can engage in meaningful conversations and activities with family and friends (Turkle, 2015).

Practical Tip. Plan regular social activities that don't involve screens, such as hiking, playing board games, or having a tech-free dinner with loved ones.

Boosts Creativity and Problem-Solving. Periodic disconnection allows your mind to wander and engage in creative thinking. Without the constant distraction of digital devices, you can explore new ideas and solutions to problems (Kounios & Beeman, 2009).

Practical Tip. Set aside time each week for activities that encourage creativity, such as brainstorming, journaling, or spending time in nature.

Implementing these strategies—managing external distractions, creating a focused environment, and incorporating digital detoxes—can help you maintain your focus in a distracting world. This approach will help you stay aligned with your goals and live a more intentional, purposeful life

5

Overcoming Obstacles to Focus

"The measure of intelligence is the ability to change."
— *Albert Einstein*

Identifying Common Challenges

Maintaining focus in a world of distractions is tough. We all face challenges that can distract us from our goals and priorities. Whether it's procrastination, fear of missing out (FOMO), or external pressures, these challenges can derail even the most well-intentioned plans. Here's an overview of these typical challenges and how to recognize when you're losing focus or drifting from your priorities.

Overview of Typical Challenges to Living a Focused Life

Procrastination is one of the most common obstacles to maintaining focus. It's the tendency to delay essential tasks in favor of more enjoyable or easier activities. While procrastination might temporarily relieve stress, it increases pressure and reduces productivity (Steel, 2007).

> ***Example.*** You know you need to start working on a project, but instead, you find yourself cleaning your desk, checking emails, or scrolling through social media. These activities feel productive at the moment, but they're distractions that prevent you from tackling the task.

Fear of Missing Out (FOMO). FOMO is the anxiety that you're missing out on something exciting or important—a social event, a career opportunity, or the latest trend. This fear can drive you to say yes to everything, even when it doesn't align with your priorities, leading to overcommitment and burnout (Przybylski et al., 2013).

> ***Example.*** You're working on an important project, but you receive an invitation to a last-minute event that everyone seems to be attending. Even though you know the project is more important, FOMO makes it hard to say no.

External Pressures. External pressures, such as expectations from family, friends, or colleagues, can also pull you away from your priorities. These pressures can manifest as the need to meet others' expectations, the desire to fit in, or the fear of disappointing someone (Deci & Ryan, 2000).

> ***Example.*** You've set aside time to work on a personal goal, but a friend asks you for help with something that isn't urgent. Even though you'd prefer to focus on your work, you feel obligated to say yes because you don't want to disappoint them.

Recognize When You're Losing Focus or Drifting from Your Priorities

Staying focused requires constant awareness of where your attention is going. Here's how to recognize when you're starting to lose focus or drift from your priorities.

Increased Procrastination. If you frequently put off important tasks, it's a sign that you're losing focus. Procrastination often occurs when tasks feel overwhelming or lack clear direction (Steel, 2007).

> *Practical Tip.* Take note of when you're procrastinating and what triggers it. Are you avoiding tasks because they're too large or unclear? Break them down into smaller, manageable steps to make them less daunting.

Feeling Overwhelmed by Options. FOMO can lead to decision paralysis, where you're so overwhelmed by options that you can't commit to any of them. You may be drifting from your priorities if you're constantly second-guessing your choices or feeling anxious about missing out (Przybylski et al., 2013).

> *Practical Tip.* Revisit your core values and priorities. Use them as a filter to make decisions, asking yourself whether an opportunity aligns with what truly matters to you.

Saying Yes Too Often. If you're saying yes to every request or opportunity, you might spread yourself too thin and lose sight of your priorities. Overcommitting is a common way people lose focus, as it diverts time and energy from what's most important (Covey, 1989).

> *Practical Tip.* Practice saying no more often, especially when a request doesn't align with your goals. Remember, every yes is also a no to something else—often something that matters more to you.

Feeling Disconnected from Your Goals. When you're drifting from your priorities, you may feel disconnected or unmotivated. Tasks that once excited you might now feel like a burden, or you may struggle to remember why you set certain goals in the first place (Dweck, 2006).

Practical Tip. Regularly revisit your goals and remind yourself why they're important. Reflect on your progress and the impact these goals will have on your life.

Noticing a Drop in Productivity. A sudden drop in productivity can indicate that you're losing focus. This might manifest as taking longer to complete tasks, making more mistakes, or constantly being busy but not making meaningful progress (González & Mark, 2004).

Practical Tip. Track your productivity over time to identify patterns. If you notice a decline, take a step back to assess where your time and energy are going and make adjustments as needed.

Recognizing these signs early can help you course-correct before you drift too far from your priorities. By staying aware of these common challenges and their symptoms, you can maintain focus and keep moving toward your goals.

Strategies for Staying on Track

Life has obstacles that can knock you off course. Whether it's procrastination, unexpected setbacks, or simply losing sight of your goals, staying on track requires intentional effort and practical strategies. Here's how to overcome these challenges, maintain momentum, and remain committed to what truly matters.

Practical Methods for Overcoming Procrastination and Maintaining Momentum

Procrastination is one of the biggest roadblocks to staying on track. Here are some practical methods to help you overcome procrastination and keep moving forward.

Break Tasks into Smaller Steps. One main reason we procrastinate is that tasks seem overwhelming. Breaking them into smaller, manageable steps makes them less daunting and easier to start (Steel, 2007).

Practical Tip. If you're procrastinating on a large project, break it down into smaller tasks that can be completed in 15-30 minutes. Start with the most straightforward task to build momentum.

Use the Two-Minute Rule. If a task will take less than two minutes to complete, do it immediately. This rule helps you overcome the initial resistance to starting a task, making it easier to build momentum (Allen, 2001).

Practical Tip. Apply the two-minute rule to small tasks like responding to an email, filing a document, or making a quick phone call. These small wins can help propel you into more significant tasks.

Visualize the Benefits of Completion. When you're struggling to get started, take a moment to visualize the benefits of completing the task. Focus on how good it will feel to have it done and how it will move you closer to your goals (Locke & Latham, 2002).

Practical Tip. Spend a few minutes visualizing the positive outcomes of completing your task, such as reduced stress, more free time, or progress toward a larger goal.

Set a Timer and Work in Sprints. The Pomodoro Technique, which involves short, focused sprints followed by brief breaks, can help you maintain momentum and avoid burnout (Cirillo, 2006).

Practical Tip. Set a timer for 25 minutes and work on a single task without interruption. When the timer goes off, take a five-minute break before starting the next session.

Staying Committed to Your Values and Priorities

Setbacks are inevitable, but they don't have to derail your progress. Here are some techniques for staying committed to your values and priorities, even when the going gets tough.

Reframe Setbacks as Learning Opportunities. Instead of viewing setbacks as failures, see them as opportunities to learn and grow. This shift in perspective can help you stay motivated and focused on your long-term goals (Dweck, 2006).

Practical Tip. When faced with a setback, ask yourself, "What can I learn from this experience? How can I use this lesson to improve moving forward?"

Revisit Your 'Why'. Your core values and priorities drive your actions. When you're discouraged or tempted to give up, revisit your 'why'—the reasons behind your goals (Simon, 2009).

Practical Tip. Write down your core values and goals and keep them where you can easily see them. When you're struggling, take a moment to reflect on why these goals matter to you.

Adjust Your Approach, Not Your Goal. If you're struggling to make progress, it may be time to adjust your approach rather than your goal. Be flexible in your methods, but stay committed to your values and priorities (Gollwitzer, 1999).

Practical Tip. If a strategy isn't working, brainstorm alternative approaches to help you reach your goal more effectively. Remember, the goal remains the same, but the path to get there may change.

Celebrate Small Wins. Recognizing and celebrating small achievements can boost your motivation and help you stay committed to your long-term goals. Each small win builds momentum and reinforces your commitment (Amabile & Kramer, 2011).

Practical Tip. Keep a journal where you record your daily accomplishments, no matter how small. Reviewing these entries can provide a sense of progress and keep you motivated.

Accountability in Staying Focused on What Truly Matters

Accountability is a powerful tool for staying on track. When you know someone else is counting on you, it's easier to stay committed to your goals and priorities. Here's how to leverage accountability to maintain focus.

Find an Accountability Partner. An accountability partner can help you stay on track by providing support, encouragement, and a sense of responsibility. Choose someone who shares your commitment to growth and will hold you accountable (Gollwitzer & Sheeran, 2006).

Practical Tip. Set up regular check-ins with your accountability partner to discuss your progress, challenges, and next steps. Knowing that someone else is monitoring your progress can increase your commitment.

Join a Group or Community. Being part of a group with similar goals can provide additional accountability and motivation. Whether it's a mastermind group, a study group, or an online community, the shared commitment can help you stay focused (Bandura, 1977).

Practical Tip. Look for groups or communities that align with your goals and values. Engage actively, share your progress, and offer support to others in the group.

Publicly Commit to Your Goals. Sharing your goals with others creates a sense of public accountability, which can increase your commitment to achieving them. The more people who know about your goals, the more motivated you'll be to stay on track (Cialdini, 2001).

Practical Tip. Announce your goals to your friends, family, or social media followers. Regularly update them on your progress to reinforce your commitment.

Use Accountability Tools. Many apps and tools are designed to help you stay accountable. These tools can track your progress, send reminders, and connect you with others who share your goals (Locke & Latham, 2002).

Practical Tip. Explore accountability apps like *Habitica*, *Beeminder*, or *StickK*. These tools can help you set goals, track progress, and stay committed to what matters most.

By implementing these strategies—overcoming procrastination, staying committed through setbacks, and leveraging accountability—you can stay on track and focus on your values and priorities. This disciplined approach will help you achieve your goals and live a life aligned with what truly matters.

Recalibrating When Necessary

Even the best-laid plans need adjustments occasionally. Life is dynamic, and your goals, priorities, and circumstances can change. Recalibrating doesn't mean you've failed; it means you're staying adaptable and intentional. Here's how to periodically assess your progress, recognize when it's time to shift focus or re-evaluate priorities and maintain flexibility without losing sight of your core values.

Assess Your Progress and Make Adjustments

Regularly assessing your progress is vital to staying on track and ensuring that your efforts align with your goals and values. Here's how to do it effectively.

Schedule Regular Check-Ins. Just as you would with a project at work, set aside time to review your personal goals and progress. Depending on your preferences, this could be weekly, monthly, or quarterly. It is important to make it a consistent habit (Schon, 1983).

Practical Tip. Block out time on your calendar at the end of each month to review your goals, assess your progress, and identify any areas that need adjustment.

Evaluate What's Working and What Isn't. During your check-ins, critically examine what's working well and what isn't. Are there certain strategies that have been particularly effective? Are there areas where you've struggled? Understanding these patterns can help refine your approach (Kolb, 1984).

Practical Tip. Use a simple SWOT[1] analysis (Strengths, Weaknesses, Opportunities, Threats) to evaluate your progress. This will help you identify areas of strength to build on and areas of weakness to address.

Set Clear Metrics for Success. It's easier to assess your progress when you have clear metrics to measure it. These could be quantitative (e.g., completing a specific number of tasks) or qualitative (e.g., feeling more aligned with your values) (Locke & Latham, 2002).

Practical Tip. For each of your goals, define what success looks like. For example, if your goal is to improve your health, your metrics might include exercising three times a week and cooking healthy meals five nights a week.

Adjust Goals and Strategies as Needed. Be willing to make adjustments based on your assessment. This might mean changing your approach, reallocating your time, or even revising your goals if they no longer align with your values or circumstances (Gollwitzer, 1999).

---

[1] SWOT analysis is a strategic planning tool used to identify an internal Strengths and Weaknesses, as well as external Opportunities and Threats. It helps to assess current position and potential future strategies by analyzing factors both within your control and in the external environment.

Practical Tip. Don't be afraid to pivot if something isn't working. If you're not progressing with a particular strategy, try a different approach to better suit your current situation.

Time to Shift Focus or Re-Evaluate Priorities?

Sometimes, despite your best efforts, you may find that your current path no longer serves you. Recognizing when it's time to shift focus or re-evaluate your priorities is crucial for long-term success and fulfillment.

Listen to Your Intuition. Your intuition is a powerful tool that can signal when something isn't right. It might be time to reassess your focus if you consistently feel uneasy, unmotivated, or disconnected from your work (Gladwell, 2005).

Practical Tip. Pay attention to how you feel about your goals and daily activities. If something feels off, reflect on whether it aligns with your values and long-term vision.

Assess Alignment with Core Values. Your core values are the foundation of your goals and decisions. If your current focus is out of alignment with these values, it's a clear sign that you must re-evaluate your priorities (Schwartz, 2012).

Practical Tip. Review and compare your core values to your current goals and activities. If there's a disconnect, consider changing to bring them back into alignment.

Identify Shifts in Your Life Circumstances. Life is full of changes—new opportunities, challenges, and responsibilities. If your circumstances have shifted, your priorities may also need to shift (Super, 1990).

Practical Tip. Reflect on any recent changes in your life, such as a new job, a change in family dynamics, or a health issue. Consider how these changes might impact your priorities and whether adjustments are needed.

Evaluate Your Long-Term Vision. Your long-term vision for your life may evolve over time. If your goals no longer align with this vision, it's time to recalibrate (Covey, 1989).

Practical Tip. Set aside time each year to reflect on your long-term vision. Ask yourself if your current goals and activities are moving you closer to that vision or if you need adjustment.

Maintaining Flexibility Without Losing Sight of Your Core Values

Staying flexible is essential for adapting to changes while staying true to your core values. Here's how to maintain flexibility without losing sight of what matters most.

Embrace a Growth Mindset. A growth mindset, the belief that you can improve and adapt through effort and learning, helps you stay open to new opportunities and challenges while remaining grounded in your values (Dweck, 2006).

Practical Tip. When faced with a challenge or setback, approach it as an opportunity to learn and grow. Ask yourself, "What can I learn from this experience, and how can I use it to move forward?"

Use a Flexible Goal-Setting Framework. Instead of rigidly sticking to one path, use a flexible goal-setting framework that allows for adjustments. SMART goals (Specific, Measurable, Achievable, Relevant, Time-bound) are a great starting point, but be willing to revise them as needed (Locke & Latham, 2002).

Practical Tip. Regularly review and update your goals to reflect changes in your circumstances or priorities. Ensure that each goal still aligns with your core values and long-term vision.

Practice Mindful Decision-Making. Mindfulness helps you stay present and make decisions that align with your values and goals, even in the face of change. It encourages you to pause, reflect, and consider the bigger picture before acting (Kabat-Zinn, 1994).

Practical Tip. Before making any significant decision, take a few moments to reflect on how it aligns with your core values and long-term goals. Consider the potential impact and whether it supports your overall vision.

Leverage Feedback and Reflection. Regular feedback and self-reflection are essential for staying on course. Seek input from trusted mentors, peers, or an accountability partner to help you stay aligned with your values while remaining adaptable (Senge, 1990).

Practical Tip. Schedule regular feedback sessions with a mentor or accountability partner. Use these sessions to discuss your progress, challenges, and necessary adjustments.

By periodically assessing your progress, recognizing when it's time to shift focus, and maintaining flexibility without losing sight of your core values, you can stay aligned with your goals and continue moving forward. This balanced approach ensures you remain adaptable while staying true to what matters.

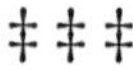

Sustaining a Life Focused on What Truly Matters

> *"It's not enough to be busy, so are the ants.*
> *The question is, what are we busy about?"*
>
> — *Henry David Thoreau*

Long-Term Strategies for Sustained Focus

Focusing on what truly matters over the long term is not just a one-time effort but an ongoing process that requires intention, reflection, and motivation. Here's how to keep your life aligned with your core values, the importance of periodic reflection, and strategies for staying motivated and inspired.

Keep Your Life Aligned with Your Core Values

Staying aligned with your core values is crucial for a fulfilling life. Here's how to ensure your actions continue to reflect what matters most to you.

Regularly Revisit Your Core Values. Life changes, and so do your perspectives. What mattered to you a decade ago might not hold the same weight today. Periodically revisiting your core values ensures that your life remains aligned with your current priorities and goals (Schwartz, 2012).

> ***Practical Tip.*** Set aside time every six months to review your core values. Ask yourself, "Do these values still resonate with me? Are my daily actions reflecting these values?"

Set Long-Term Goals That Reflect Your Values. Long-term goals serve as a roadmap, guiding your actions and decisions. Ensure these goals align with your core values to make every step meaningful and purposeful (Locke & Latham, 2002).

> ***Practical Tip.*** Set one or two long-term goals for each core value. For example, if health is a core value, a long-term goal might be maintaining a balanced lifestyle that includes regular exercise, healthy eating, and stress management.

Stay Flexible Yet Focused. While staying focused on your long-term goals is essential, life is unpredictable. Flexibility allows you to adapt to changes without losing sight of your core values (Dweck, 2006).

> ***Practical Tip.*** When life throws you a curveball, revisit your goals and values. Adjust your strategies as needed, but stay committed to the underlying principles that guide you.

Periodic Reflection and Reassessment

Periodic reflection is essential for aligning your core values and long-term goals. It allows you to assess your progress, make necessary adjustments, and stay on track.

> **Conduct Regular Self-Assessments.** Reflecting on your actions and decisions helps you understand whether they bring you closer to your goals. Regular self-assessments ensure you're not drifting away from your priorities (Schon, 1983).

> ***Practical Tip.*** At the end of each month, spend 15-20 minutes reflecting on your progress. Ask yourself, "Am I living in

alignment with my values? What adjustments do I need to make?"

Reassess Your Goals Periodically. As you grow and evolve, your goals may need reassessment. Periodic goal reassessment helps you stay relevant and focused on what truly matters (Kolb, 1984).

Practical Tip. Once a year, review your long-term goals. Evaluate whether they still align with your current values and life circumstances. Make adjustments as necessary to stay on course.

Seek Feedback from Trusted Sources. Sometimes, it's hard to see the bigger picture alone. Seeking feedback from mentors, peers, or loved ones can provide valuable insights and help you reassess your path (Senge, 1990).

Practical Tip. Schedule regular check-ins with a mentor or accountability partner to discuss your progress and receive constructive feedback.

Staying Motivated and Inspired

Maintaining focus over the long term requires ongoing motivation and inspiration. Here are some strategies to keep your drive alive.

Celebrate Small Wins. Recognizing and celebrating small achievements keeps you motivated and reinforces your commitment to your goals (Amabile & Kramer, 2011).

Practical Tip. Keep a journal where you record your achievements, no matter how small. Review these entries regularly to remind yourself of your progress.

Stay Connected to Your 'Why'. Understanding the deeper reasons behind your goals provides a powerful source of motivation. Stay connected to your 'why' to maintain focus and drive (Simon, 2009).

Practical Tip. Write down why your goals are important to you. Revisit this list whenever you feel your motivation waning.

Incorporate Regular Inspiration into Your Routine. Surround yourself with sources of inspiration that keep you motivated. This could be books, podcasts, or people who embody the values you aspire to live by (Duhigg, 2012).

> ***Practical Tip.*** Dedicate time each week to reading or listening to something that inspires you. This regular dose of inspiration can help you stay energized and focused on your long-term goals.

Visualize Your Success. Visualization is a powerful tool that can keep you motivated by helping you see the positive outcomes of your efforts. Regularly visualizing your success can reinforce your commitment to your goals (Locke & Latham, 2002).

> ***Practical Tip.*** Spend a few minutes each day visualizing yourself achieving your goals. Imagine the positive impact this success will have on your life and the lives of those around you.

You can sustain long-term focus on what truly matters by following these strategies—regularly revisiting your core values, conducting periodic reflection and reassessment, and staying motivated. This disciplined approach ensures that your life remains aligned with your values, leading to a fulfilling and purpose-driven existence.

Integrating Focus into Every Aspect of Life

Focus isn't just for your work or big goals—it's a principle that can be applied across every aspect of your life. When you integrate focus into your health, relationships, and even leisure, you create a balanced, purpose-driven life that benefits you and positively impacts those around you. Here's how to make focus a foundational element of your daily living.

Applying the Principles of Focus Across Different Areas of Your Life

Applying focus to different aspects of your life requires intentionality. Here's how you can integrate this principle into key areas.

Health and Well-Being. Your physical and mental health are foundational to everything else in your life. Focusing on healthy habits sets the stage for sustained energy and resilience (Clear, 2018).

Practical Tip. Prioritize daily activities that enhance your well-being, such as regular exercise, healthy eating, and sufficient sleep. Schedule these activities with the same importance as your work commitments.

Relationships. Meaningful relationships require attention and presence. By focusing on the quality of your interactions rather than the quantity, you can deepen your connections and improve your relationships (Chapman, 1995).

Practical Tip. Set aside dedicated time for the important people in your life. During this time, be fully present—put away your devices, listen actively, and engage in meaningful conversations.

Leisure and Recreation. Leisure time is crucial for relaxation and rejuvenation, but it's easy to let it become a distraction rather than a source of renewal. Focused leisure activities can enhance creativity and well-being (Csikszentmihalyi, 1990).

Practical Tip. Choose leisure activities that truly refresh you and align with your values, such as reading, spending time in nature, or engaging in a hobby. Avoid passive activities that leave you feeling drained.

Personal Growth. Continuous personal growth keeps you engaged and motivated. Focus on learning and experiences that align with your core values and contribute to your long-term goals (Dweck, 2006).

Practical Tip. Set aside weekly time for personal development, such as reading, taking courses, or practicing new skills. Focus on growth areas that resonate with your values and life goals.

Balancing Work, Relationships, and Personal Growth Without Compromising Focus

Balancing work, relationships, and personal growth demands can be challenging, but it's essential for a well-rounded life. Here's how to maintain that balance without losing focus.

Prioritize and Align Your Activities. The key to balance is prioritization. Align your daily activities with your core values and long-term goals. This ensures you're spending time on what truly matters (Covey, 1989).

Practical Tip. Use a weekly planner to map out your time. Allocate specific blocks for work, relationships, personal growth, and leisure. Make sure each area gets the attention it deserves without overwhelming your schedule.

Set Boundaries. Clear boundaries help you protect your focus across different areas of your life. This means knowing when to say no and when to step back to maintain balance (Newport, 2016).

Practical Tip. Establish boundaries around work hours, personal time, and relationships. For example, set a cut-off time for work each day to ensure you have time for family and personal growth.

Practice Mindful Transitions. Moving from one activity to another can cause stress and scatter your focus. Mindful transitions help you shift gears smoothly and maintain focus in each area of your life (Kabat-Zinn, 1994).

Practical Tip. Take a few deep breaths or a short walk between work and personal time. Use this transition to clear your mind and refocus on the next activity.

Avoid Multitasking. Multitasking dilutes your focus and reduces the quality of your work and relationships. Focus on one thing at a time to maintain balance and achieve better results (González & Mark, 2004).

Practical Tip. When working, focus solely on work. When spending time with loved ones, give them your full attention. This single-tasking approach enhances both productivity and connection.

The Ripple Effect. How Living a Focused Life Benefits Those Around You

When you live a focused life, the benefits extend beyond yourself. Here's how your focus can positively impact those around you.

Setting an Example. By living a focused and balanced life, you set a positive example for others. Your actions show that achieving success and fulfillment is possible without sacrificing well-being or relationships (Covey, 1989).

Practical Tip. Share your strategies for maintaining focus and balance with others. Encourage friends, family, and colleagues to adopt similar practices.

Improving Relationships. When you're focused and present in your relationships, the quality of your interactions improves. This deepens your connections and creates a positive environment for those around you (Chapman, 1995).

Practical Tip. Practice active listening and empathy in your interactions. Show genuine interest in others, and your relationships will thrive.

Contributing to a Positive Work Environment. A focused and balanced approach to work can inspire your colleagues and contribute to a more productive and positive work environment (Pink, 2009).

Practical Tip. Share your focus strategies with your team. Encourage time blocking, mindful transitions, and boundary-setting to enhance productivity and well-being.

Creating a Supportive Community. Living a focused life can inspire others to do the same, leading to a supportive community where everyone strives to live according to their values and goals (Bandura, 1977).

Practical Tip. Engage with like-minded individuals who share your commitment to focus and balance. Support each other in maintaining these principles and create a community that fosters growth and well-being.

By integrating focus into every aspect of your life—from health to leisure, from work to relationships—you create a balanced, purpose-driven life that benefits you and positively impacts those around you. This holistic approach ensures that your focus is not limited to one area but is a guiding principle that shapes your entire life.

Leaving a Legacy

A life focused on what truly matters doesn't just benefit you in the present—it creates a lasting impact that can resonate long after you're gone. Leaving a legacy is about reflecting on the impact of your actions, ensuring that what you do today has a positive effect on the future, and sharing your journey and insights with others. Here's how to think about and work towards leaving a meaningful legacy.

Reflecting on the Impact of a Life Well-Lived, Focused on What Truly Matters

Your legacy is built on your choices and how you live your life. A life well-lived, focused on what truly matters, naturally creates a legacy that others will remember and benefit from.

Consider the Long-Term Impact of Your Actions. Every action you take has a ripple effect. Reflect on how your decisions and behavior influence your life, the lives of those around you, and the broader community (Covey, 1989).

Practical Tip. Take time to reflect on your daily actions. Ask yourself, "How will this decision impact others? What kind of example am I setting for those who look up to me?"

Align Your Life with Your Core Values. When your actions consistently align with your core values, you create a legacy that reflects what's most important to you. This alignment ensures that your life's work is meaningful and impactful (Schwartz, 2012).

Practical Tip. Regularly review your core values and ensure your goals and actions align with them. This alignment will naturally guide you toward creating a legacy that matters.

Focus on Contributions Rather Than Accumulations. A lasting legacy isn't about what you acquire but what you contribute. Consider how your talents, time, and resources can be used to make a difference in the lives of others (Sinek, 2009).

Practical Tip. Identify ways to contribute to your community or causes you care about. This could be through mentoring, volunteering, or supporting organizations that align with your values.

Ensure That Your Actions Today Create a Lasting, Positive Impact

Leaving a legacy requires intentionality. Here's how to ensure that your actions today are paving the way for a positive and enduring impact.

Be Intentional with Your Time and Energy. Your time and energy are your most valuable resources. Use them wisely by focusing on activities that align with your long-term vision and values (Clear, 2018).

Practical Tip. Prioritize your activities based on their long-term impact. Spend more time on what truly matters and less on distractions or activities that don't contribute to your legacy.

Invest in Relationships. The relationships you build and nurture will be a significant part of your legacy. The time and effort you invest in others can create a lasting positive impact in their lives and the broader community (Chapman, 1995).

> ***Practical Tip.*** Make a conscious effort to build solid and meaningful relationships. Offer support, guidance, and encouragement to those around you, and be a positive influence in their lives.

Create and Share Value. Whether through your work, your personal life, or your community involvement, focus on creating and sharing value. This could be through knowledge, resources, or support that helps others grow and succeed (Senge, 1990).

> ***Practical Tip.*** Look for opportunities to share your knowledge and experiences with others. This could be through teaching, writing, or simply offering advice and support to those who need it.

Plan for the Future. A legacy doesn't happen by accident. It requires planning and foresight. Consider how you want to be remembered and what steps you must take to make that vision a reality (Locke & Latham, 2002).

> ***Practical Tip.*** Create a legacy plan that outlines your long-term goals and the steps you need to take to achieve them. This plan could include financial planning, mentoring, or creating a charitable foundation.

Share Your Journey and Insights with Others

Your experiences and insights are valuable, not just to you but to others who can learn from your journey. Sharing your story can inspire and guide others, helping them to live more focused, meaningful lives.

Be Open About Your Journey. Sharing the challenges and successes of your journey can provide valuable lessons for others. Don't be afraid to speak about your experiences and what you've learned (Dweck, 2006).

Practical Tip. Consider writing about your experiences in a blog, journal, or book. Share your insights in conversations, talks, or social media to reach a broader audience.

Mentor and Guide Others. One of the most direct ways to share your journey is through mentoring. By guiding others, you help them navigate their paths and build their legacies (Bandura, 1977).

Practical Tip. Offer to mentor someone who could benefit from your experience. This could be a younger colleague, a student, or a community member.

Create a Platform for Sharing. If you're passionate about your journey and want to reach a larger audience, consider creating a platform to share your insights. This could be through a podcast, YouTube channel, or online community (Pink, 2009).

Practical Tip. Choose a medium that suits your strengths and start sharing your story. Engage with your audience and encourage others to share their journeys as well.

Encourage Others to Reflect on Their Legacy. Inspire others to think about the legacy they want to leave. By fostering a culture of reflection and intentional living, you contribute to a community that values long-term impact (Covey, 1989).

Practical Tip. Ask others about their goals and how they want to be remembered in conversations. Encourage them to reflect on their legacy and take steps toward building it.

By reflecting on the impact of a life well-lived, ensuring that your actions today create a lasting, positive impact, and sharing your journey with others, you can leave a meaningful legacy that benefits future generations. This intentional approach to living and leading by example will help you create a legacy that truly matters.

‡ ‡ ‡

7

The Power of Living with Focus

"It is not the mountain we conquer, but ourselves."
— Sir Edmund Hillary

Summary of Key Insights

Throughout this book, we've explored what it means to live a life focused on what truly matters. We've covered practical strategies for maintaining focus in a world full of distractions, staying true to your core values, and ensuring your daily actions align with your long-term goals. Here's a recap of the most important lessons and strategies we've discussed and a final reinforcement of why living with focus is crucial.

Lessons and Strategies from the Book

Clarifying Your Core Values. Everything starts with clearly understanding your core values. These are the principles that guide your decisions and actions. Without a strong foundation in your values, external pressures and distractions make it easy to get sidetracked. We discussed identifying and prioritizing these values, ensuring that they serve as your North Star in all areas of life (Schwartz, 2012).

> ***Key Takeaway.*** Regularly revisit your core values to ensure your goals and actions align with what matters most to you.

Setting Life Priorities. Once you're clear on your values, the next step is to set priorities that reflect them. This involves making tough decisions about where to focus your time and energy. We explored techniques for ranking and balancing priorities across different areas of life, such as work, relationships, and personal growth (Covey, 1989).

> ***Key Takeaway.*** Use your core values as a filter to decide where to direct your focus. Prioritize activities that align with your long-term goals and contribute to your overall well-being.

Managing Time Effectively. Time management is critical for maintaining focus. We delved into practical methods like time blocking, setting clear boundaries, and avoiding common time-wasters. These strategies help ensure you dedicate your time to what truly matters (Newport, 2016).

> ***Key Takeaway.*** Treat your time as a valuable resource. Schedule your day with intention, focusing on high-priority tasks and minimizing distractions.

Building Resilience and Staying Motivated. Staying focused isn't always easy—life is full of challenges and setbacks. We discussed strategies for building mental resilience, such as cultivating a growth mindset and celebrating small wins. These practices motivate you and help you stay on track, even when things get tough (Dweck, 2006).

> ***Key Takeaway.*** Resilience and motivation are crucial to sustaining focus over the long term. Embrace challenges as opportunities to grow, and celebrate your progress.

Recalibrating When Necessary. Life is dynamic, and your priorities and goals may need to shift over time. We discussed the importance of regularly assessing your progress and adjusting as needed. Flexibility and a clear sense of direction ensure you remain aligned with your core values, even as circumstances change (Kolb, 1984).

Key Takeaway. Periodically reassess your goals and strategies to ensure they align with your values. Don't be afraid to adjust your approach when necessary.

Importance of Living a Life Focused on What Truly Matters

Living a focused life isn't just about achieving goals—it's about ensuring that your daily life aligns with your deepest values and highest priorities. When you live with focus, you're not just more productive—you're more fulfilled. You can build meaningful relationships, make significant contributions, and leave a lasting legacy. Living a life focused on what truly matters is your greatest tool for creating a life of purpose and impact in a world filled with distractions.

Remember, the strategies and lessons in this book are not one-time fixes—they're ongoing practices. The more you integrate them into your daily life, the more natural they will become, leading to a more intentional, focused, and fulfilling life.

Final Words of Encouragement

You've read the book, absorbed the principles, and now it's time to take action. The strategies and insights you've gained won't make a difference unless you apply them. So, here's your challenge. Start now. Not tomorrow, not next week—now. Because the sooner you begin to implement these principles, the sooner you'll start to see the benefits in your life.

Take Immediate Action

Don't let this book become just another item on your shelf. The ideas we've explored together are meant to be lived, not just read. If you're serious about living a life focused on what truly matters, the time to act is now. Start with a tiny change—setting clearer priorities, eliminating distractions, or simply revisiting your core values. Small steps taken consistently can lead to profound transformations.

> ***Practical Tip.*** Choose one principle from this book that resonated most with you and apply it today. Maybe it's time-blocking, setting boundaries, or focusing on your core values. Whatever it is, take that first step now.

A More Meaningful, Fulfilled Life Through Focus

Here's the bottom line. Living a focused life isn't just about productivity or success—it's about living with purpose. When you align your actions with your values and focus on what truly matters, you create a life rich with meaning. You'll find that your days are more satisfying, your relationships are deeper, and your contributions are more impactful.

By focusing on what matters most, you're not just achieving goals—you're building a legacy, creating a life of significance, and setting an example for others to follow. This is the promise of living with focus. a life that's not only successful but deeply fulfilling.

So, as you close this book, remember that you have the power to live a focused life. The decisions you make today will shape your tomorrow. Stay committed, stay focused, and watch as your life transforms into something truly remarkable.

Suggested Next Steps

> **Revisit Your Core Values.** Take some time to reflect on your core values and how they align with your current goals. Make any necessary adjustments to ensure your actions reflect what truly matters.

Set Clear, Focused Goals. Identify one or two key goals that align with your core values. Break them down into actionable steps and start working on them immediately.

Create a Routine That Supports Focus. Design a daily routine that prioritizes your most important tasks and minimizes distractions. Stick to it consistently.

Reflect and Adjust Regularly. Schedule regular check-ins to assess your progress and adjust as needed. Stay flexible but focused on your long-term vision.

Share Your Journey. Inspire others by sharing your journey toward a more focused life. Whether through conversations, social media, or writing, let others see the impact of living with focus.

You have everything you need to live a focused, meaningful, and fulfilled life. Now, it's time to make it happen. Start today and keep moving forward. The best is yet to come.

Call to Action

It's time to turn everything you've learned into action. Knowledge without action is just potential waiting to be realized. To fully benefit from the principles in this book, you need to integrate them into your daily life. Here's how you can start making these changes today.

Integrating the Book's Teachings into Daily Life

Start with a Morning Routine. Your morning sets the tone for the rest of your day. Begin each day with a focused, intentional routine that aligns with your core values and goals. This could include practices like meditation, journaling, exercise, or reviewing your priorities for the day (Hal Elrod, 2012).

Action Step. Design a morning routine with at least one activity that helps you focus on your goals. Commit to this routine for 30 days and observe how it impacts your daily focus.

Implement Time Blocking. Time Blocking is a powerful tool for ensuring that your most important tasks get done. Allocate specific blocks of time in your day for focused work, free from distractions. This helps you stay on track and ensures your priorities are always front and center (Newport, 2016).

Action Step. Plan your day using time blocks. Start with your most critical tasks and ensure you have time to work on them uninterrupted. Stick to these time blocks as closely as possible.

Regularly Revisit and Reaffirm Your Core Values. Your core values are the foundation of a focused life. Regularly revisiting them helps you stay aligned and ensures that your actions reflect what truly matters to you. Make it a habit to reflect on your values and adjust your goals and actions accordingly (Schwartz, 2012).

Action Step. Schedule a monthly review session where you revisit your core values and assess whether your recent actions and decisions align with them. Adjust your plans as necessary.

Eliminate Distractions. Distractions are the enemy of focus. Identify the biggest distractions in your life—social media, excessive multitasking, or other time-wasters—and take steps to minimize or eliminate them (Clear, 2018).

Action Step. Identify one major distraction that's hindering your focus. Take immediate steps to reduce or eliminate it, such as using apps that block distracting websites during work hours or setting specific times for checking emails and messages.

Reflect and Adjust Weekly. A weekly reflection session allows you to review your progress, celebrate your wins, and make any necessary adjustments. This practice keeps you on track and helps you stay focused on your long-term goals (Schon, 1983).

Action Step. Set aside 15-30 minutes at the end of each week for reflection. Ask yourself what went well, what didn't, and how you can improve in the coming week. Use this time to plan your next steps and reinforce your commitment to your goals.

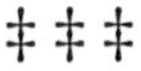

Appendix - A

Action Plan. Living with Focus and Purpose

This action plan is designed to help you apply the principles and strategies from the book Getting Down to Brass Tacks to your daily life. By following these steps, you'll be able to live with greater focus, align your actions with your core values, and achieve your goals with clarity and purpose.

Action Plan Overview

Phase One. Clarify Your Core Values

Objective. Identify and articulate the core values that guide your life.

Phase Two. Set Your Life Priorities

Objective. Align your daily actions with your core values by setting clear priorities.

Phase Three: Eliminate the Non-Essential

Objective. Remove distractions and unnecessary obligations that do not align with your core values.

Phase Four. Develop a Focused Mindset

Objective. Cultivate the mental resilience and focus needed to achieve your goals.

Phase Five. Create Effective Routines

Objective. Establish daily routines that support a life focused on what truly matters.

Phase Six. Stay Grounded in Your Purpose

Objective. Remain connected to your core values and long-term goals, even amidst challenges.

Phase Seven. Build a Legacy

Objective. Create a life that leaves a positive, lasting impact.

Following this action plan, you can systematically apply the Getting Down to Brass Tacks principles to your life. Stay committed to your core values, set clear priorities, and eliminate distractions to live a focused, intentional life. Remember, this journey is ongoing, and it's essential to remain flexible and open to growth as you pursue a life that truly matters.

§

Action Plan
Phase One

Clarifying Your Core Values

Objective. The goal of this exercise is to help you identify and clearly articulate the core values that guide your life. Your core values are the fundamental beliefs that shape your decisions, actions, and, ultimately, the course of your life. By understanding and prioritizing these values, you can live a more focused and intentional life.

Step 1. Reflect on Peak Experiences

Purpose. This exercise helps you identify your core values by reflecting on moments in your life when you felt most fulfilled, proud, or content. These experiences often reveal the values that matter most to you.

How to Do It.

Find a Quiet Space. Set aside some uninterrupted time in a quiet space where you can reflect deeply. Bring a journal or a piece of paper to write down your thoughts.

Recall Meaningful Moments. Think about three to five moments in your life when you felt exceptionally fulfilled, proud, or content. These could be personal achievements, times of deep connection with others, or moments of significant personal growth.

Identify the Themes. For each moment, ask yourself the following questions.

What was happening?

Who were you with?

What emotions were you experiencing?

What made this moment so meaningful?

Write down the themes or values that these moments highlight. For example, a core value might be compassion or service if a peak experience involved helping someone in need.

List Your Values. Based on your reflections, list the values that repeatedly appear in your peak experiences. These are likely to be some of your core values.

Step 2. Daily Choices Analysis

Purpose. Your daily choices—how you spend your time, energy, and money—can reveal what you truly value, sometimes more accurately than what you think you value.

How to Do It.

Track Your Time and Spending. For one week, keep a detailed log of how you spend your time and money. Break down your day into activities and note how much time you dedicate to each. Similarly, track your expenditures, including what you spend on and why.

Analyze Your Patterns. At the end of the week, review your log. Consider the following questions.

What activities or expenditures took up most of your time and money?

Which of these made you feel fulfilled or satisfied?

Which activities or expenditures seemed like a waste of time or money?

The activities that align with what you enjoy and find meaningful are often linked to your core values. For instance, if you spend a lot of time volunteering, you might value community service or altruism.

List Your Values. From your analysis, list the values that your daily choices reflect. Compare this list with the values you identified in Step 1 to see if there are overlaps or new insights.

Step 3. Prioritize Your Values

Purpose. Not all values hold the same weight in your life. Prioritizing them helps you understand which values are most central to your identity and decision-making process.

How to Do It.

Review Your Values. Look at the list of values you've identified from Steps 1 and 2. Write them down in no particular order.

Rank Your Values. Rank these values in order of importance. Ask yourself.

Which value would I never compromise on?

If two values were in conflict, which one would I prioritize?

This process may be challenging, but it's essential to understand which values guide your most critical decisions. For example, if you value both family and career, but in a conflict, you'd prioritize family, then family ranks higher.

Create a Final List. Create a final list of your top 5-7 core values, ranked in order of importance. This list will serve as your compass for making decisions and setting priorities in life.

Step 4. Articulate Your Values

Purpose. Writing a statement for each value helps clarify why each one is important to you and how it influences your life. This step turns abstract concepts into concrete principles that guide your actions.

How to Do It.

Write a Value Statement. For each of your top values, write a brief statement that answers the following questions.

Why is this value important to me?

How does this value influence my decisions and actions?

What are some examples of how I live this value?

For example, if one of your values is integrity, your statement might look like this. "Integrity is important to me because it ensures that I am honest and trustworthy in all my interactions. It influences my decisions by guiding me to choose the right path, even when it's difficult. I live this value by being transparent in my communications and holding myself accountable to my commitments."

Review and Reflect. Once you've written a statement for each value, review them regularly. Reflect on how these values manifest in your daily life and consider how they might guide future decisions.

Integrate Into Your Life. Keep your value statements visible—perhaps in a journal, on your phone, or on a bulletin board. Refer to them when making decisions or setting goals to ensure that your actions align with your core values.

Final Thoughts.

Clarifying your core values is a powerful exercise that lays the foundation for a focused, intentional life. By understanding what truly matters to you, you can make decisions that align with your values, prioritize your time and energy effectively, and live a life that is authentically yours.

Sample Journal Entries

Location. My Study Room   Date. August 24, 2024
Mood. Reflective, Calm

Recalling Meaningful Moments

Moment #1. My college graduation day.

Moment #2. Volunteering at a local shelter during a particularly cold winter.

Moment #3. Completing my first marathon.

Identifying Themes / Core Valse

Moment #1. My college graduation day.

What was happening? I was walking across the stage to receive my diploma.

Who was with me? My family and close friends were in the audience, cheering me on.

What emotions was I experiencing? A mix of pride, relief, and deep satisfaction.

What made this moment so meaningful? This moment marked the culmination of years of hard work, perseverance, and the support of those I love.

Common Themes/Values. Achievement, Family Support, Perseverance

...

Moment #2. Volunteering at a local shelter during a particularly cold winter.

What was happening? I was distributing warm meals and blankets to those in need.

Who was with me? A group of fellow volunteers who shared my commitment to helping others.

What emotions was I experiencing? Compassion, a sense of purpose, and connection with others.

What made this moment so meaningful? Seeing the immediate impact of our efforts on the lives of those we were helping gave me a profound sense of purpose.

Common Themes/Values. Compassion, Service, Community.

...

Moment #3. Completing my first marathon.

What was happening? Crossing the finish line after months of training.

Who was with me? My running group, who had trained with me, and my family cheering me on.

What emotions was I experiencing? Elation, exhaustion, pride.

What made this moment so meaningful? It represented the achievement of a long-term goal and the physical and mental endurance it took to get there.

Common Themes/Values. Determination, Health, Achievement.

The Core Values I Identified.

Achievement	Family Support	Perseverance
Compassion	Service	Community
Determination	Health	

Personal Reflection.

Through this exercise, I've identified that achievement, compassion, and community are central to my sense of fulfillment. I'll prioritize these values in my decision-making and goal-setting processes.

Action Plan
Phase Two

Setting Your Life Priorities

Objective. The goal of this guide is to help you align your daily actions with your core values by setting clear, intentional priorities. By identifying the most important areas of your life and linking them to your core values, you can ensure that your time and energy are focused on what truly matters.

Step 1: Identify Key Life Areas

Purpose. Before you can set priorities, you need to define the main areas of your life that require your attention and effort. These areas represent different aspects of your life that are essential to your well-being and fulfillment.

How to Do It:

List Your Key Life Areas: Begin by listing the major areas of your life that require your focus. Common areas include:

Family: Relationships with your spouse, children, parents, or extended family.

Career: Your job, business, or professional development.

Health: Physical well-being, fitness, nutrition, and mental health.

Personal Growth: Learning, self-improvement, hobbies, and spiritual growth.

Social Life: Friendships, community involvement, and social activities.

Finances: Budgeting, saving, investing, and financial planning.

Recreation: Leisure activities, hobbies, and relaxation.

Reflect on the Importance of Each Area: Consider how each area impacts your overall well-being and fulfillment. Ask yourself:

Which areas are currently demanding the most attention?

Which areas, if neglected, would cause the most dissatisfaction or stress?

Create Your List: Write down your key life areas, making sure to capture all aspects that are significant to you. This list will serve as the foundation for setting your priorities.

Step 2: Link to Core Values

Purpose: Connecting each key life area to your core values ensures that your priorities are rooted in what truly matters to you. This alignment helps you make decisions that are consistent with your values, leading to a more purposeful life.

How to Do It:

Review Your Core Values: Revisit the core values you identified in the previous exercise. These values should serve as guiding principles for your priorities.

Match Values to Life Areas: For each key life area, identify which of your core values it reflects. For example:

Family: This might connect to values like love, connection, or responsibility.

Career: This could reflect values such as achievement, integrity, or innovation.

Health: This may be tied to values like vitality, balance, or self-care.

Write Down the Connections: Create a clear connection between each life area and your core values. For example:

"Family is important to me because it aligns with my value of love and connection. Prioritizing time with my family strengthens these bonds and fulfills my desire for meaningful relationships."

Reflect on Alignment: Take a moment to reflect on how well your current life areas align with your core values. Are there areas where you're spending time that don't reflect your values? Are there values that aren't being expressed through your daily activities?

Step 3: Rank Your Priorities

Purpose: Ranking your priorities helps you determine where to focus your time and energy, ensuring that the most important areas of your life receive the attention they deserve.

How to Do It:

Rank the Key Areas: Review your list of key life areas and rank them in order of importance based on your current circumstances and core values. Consider the following questions:

Which areas need the most attention right now?

Where do you need to make the most significant changes or improvements?

Which areas are most aligned with your core values?

Focus on the Top 3-5 Areas: While all life areas are important, focusing on the top 3-5 will help you make meaningful progress without feeling overwhelmed. For example, if your top priorities are family, career, and health, these should be the areas where you dedicate most of your time and energy.

Document Your Priorities: Write down your ranked priorities, ensuring that they are clear and actionable. For example:

Family: Spend quality time with my spouse and children daily.

Career: Focus on professional development and achieving key work milestones.

Health: Commit to a regular exercise routine and healthy eating."

Step 4: Balance Your Priorities

Purpose: Balancing your priorities ensures that you allocate your time effectively across the different areas of your life. This step helps you avoid overcommitting to one area at the expense of others.

How to Do It:

Time Blocking: Time blocking involves setting aside specific blocks of time for each priority. This technique ensures that each area gets the attention it deserves without overwhelming you.

Create a Weekly Schedule: Block out time in your calendar for each of your top priorities. For example, you might dedicate weekday mornings to exercise (health), evenings to family time, and certain afternoons to professional development.

Stick to Your Blocks: Treat these blocks as non-negotiable appointments. By doing so, you prevent other less important tasks from encroaching on your priorities.

Use the Eisenhower Matrix: The Eisenhower Matrix is a tool that helps you prioritize tasks based on urgency and importance. This matrix has four quadrants:

Urgent and Important: Tasks you should do immediately.

Important, Not Urgent: Tasks you should schedule for later.

Urgent, Not Important: Tasks you should delegate if possible.

Not Urgent, Not Important: Tasks you should eliminate.

Apply this matrix to your tasks and activities within each key life area to ensure that your time is spent on what truly matters.

Eisenhower Matrix

	Urgent	Not Urgent
	Do Now	**Schedule**
Important	- Complete client report (due today) - Respond to urgent customer emails	- Plan long-term project - Exercise/health routine - Strategic business planning
	Delegate	**Eliminate**
Not Important	- Schedule team meetings - Handle routine requests - Answer non-essential emails	- Scroll through social media - Unnecessary meetings - Watching TV shows without purpose

Avoid Overcommitting: Balance isn't about doing everything equally; it's about giving the right amount of attention to the right things. Be realistic about how much you can handle, and don't hesitate to say no to commitments that don't align with your priorities.

Step 5: Be Flexible

Purpose: Priorities can change over time due to life's evolving nature. Regularly revisiting and adjusting your priorities ensures they remain aligned with your current values and circumstances.

How to Do It:

Schedule Regular Check-Ins: Set aside time—monthly, quarterly, or annually—to review your priorities. Reflect on questions such as:

Are my priorities still aligned with my core values?

Have any life changes impacted my priorities?

Do I need to adjust how I'm allocating my time?

Adapt to Life's Changes: Life is dynamic, and so are your priorities. When significant life events occur (e.g., a new job, the birth of a child, a health issue), be willing to adjust your priorities accordingly. This flexibility ensures that you stay aligned with what truly matters.

Reaffirm Your Core Values: As part of your check-in, revisit your core values to ensure they still resonate with you. If your values have evolved, update your priorities to reflect these changes.

Embrace Change: Understand that shifting priorities is a natural part of life. Embrace these changes as opportunities for growth and realignment with your values. Flexibility allows you to respond to life's challenges and opportunities with resilience and intention.

Final Thoughts:

Setting your life priorities is an ongoing process that requires reflection, intentionality, and flexibility. By following these steps, you can ensure that your daily actions are aligned with your core values, leading to a more focused, balanced, and fulfilling life.

§

Phase Three

Eliminating the Non-Essential

Objective: The goal of this guide is to help you remove distractions and unnecessary obligations from your life, allowing you to focus on what truly matters. By eliminating the non-essential, you can align your actions more closely with your core values and priorities.

Step 1: Identify Distractions

Purpose: To effectively eliminate the non-essential, you first need to identify the activities and commitments that distract you from your goals and values. Tracking how you spend your time will provide insight into where your energy is being drained by non-essential tasks.

How to Do It:

Track Your Time:

Use a Time Journal: For one week, keep a detailed journal of how you spend your time each day. Include everything—work tasks, meetings, social media use, chores, and downtime.

Categorize Your Activities: At the end of the week, review your journal and categorize each activity as either essential or non-essential. Essential activities are those that align with your core values and priorities, while non-essential activities are those that do not.

Analyze the Results:

Identify Patterns: Look for patterns in your time journal. Are there certain activities or times of day when you are most prone to distractions? Are there commitments that take up significant time but don't contribute to your priorities?

Assess the Impact: Consider the impact of these non-essential activities on your life. Are they causing stress, reducing productivity, or pulling you away from what truly matters?

Create an Action Plan:

List Non-Essential Activities: Make a list of the non-essential activities you've identified. Decide which ones you can reduce, delegate, or eliminate altogether.

Set Boundaries: Establish clear boundaries to prevent these non-essential activities from creeping back into your schedule. For example, set specific times for checking emails or limit social media use to certain hours.

Step 2: Declutter Your Environment

Purpose: A cluttered environment—both physical and mental—can make it difficult to focus on what's truly important. Simplifying your surroundings and limiting the information you consume can help you maintain clarity and focus.

How to Do It:

Physical Decluttering:

Start Small: Begin with a single area, such as your workspace or a specific room in your home. Remove items that you no longer use, need, or love.

Adopt the "One In, One Out" Rule: For every new item you bring into your space, eliminate something else. This helps maintain a clutter-free environment and prevents the accumulation of unnecessary stuff.

Organize by Function: Arrange your belongings in a way that supports your priorities. For example, if learning and personal growth are important to you, create a dedicated reading or study area free from distractions.

Mental Decluttering:

Limit Information Intake: Be selective about the information you consume. Avoid overwhelming yourself with news, social media, or other content that doesn't add value to your life.

Practice Mindfulness: Mindfulness is a powerful tool for clearing mental clutter. Spend a few minutes each day practicing mindfulness or meditation to stay present and focused.

Resolve Unfinished Business: Unresolved issues, whether they're personal or professional, can take up mental space and drain your energy. Make a plan to address these issues, whether that means having a difficult conversation, completing a lingering task, or letting go of something that no longer serves you.

Create a Calm Environment:

Simplify Your Digital Space: Declutter your digital environment by organizing files, unsubscribing from unnecessary emails, and limiting notifications. A clean digital workspace can reduce mental overload.

Incorporate Elements of Nature: Adding natural elements to your space, such as plants or natural light, can enhance your environment and promote a sense of calm and focus.

Step 3: Practice Saying No

Purpose: Learning to say no is crucial for protecting your time and energy. By declining tasks or commitments that don't align with your priorities, you can focus on what truly matters and prevent burnout.

How to Do It:

Know Your Priorities:

Revisit Your Core Values: Before making a decision, consider how it aligns with your core values and priorities. If a request doesn't support your goals, it's okay to decline.

Create a Decision-Making Framework: Develop a simple framework for making decisions. For example, ask yourself: "Does this align with my top priorities? Will it bring me closer to my goals? Do I have the time and energy to commit to this?"

Be Direct and Honest:

Practice a Polite Decline: Saying no doesn't have to be difficult. Practice polite but firm responses such as, "Thank you for thinking of me, but I'm focusing on other commitments right now," or "I appreciate the opportunity, but this doesn't align with my current priorities."

Avoid Over-Explaining: You don't need to provide lengthy explanations for your decisions. A simple, honest response is often enough.

Start Small:

Practice in Low-Stakes Situations: If saying no feels uncomfortable, start by practicing in situations with lower stakes. As you become more confident, you'll find it easier to say no when it counts.

Offer Alternatives: If you feel compelled to help but can't commit, offer an alternative solution. For example, you might suggest someone else who's better suited for the task or offer to help at a later time when it fits your schedule.

Recognize the Long-Term Benefits:

Protect Your Time: Remember that saying no today allows you to say yes to the things that truly matter in the long run. Whenever you say no to a distraction or unnecessary obligation, you're making space for the priorities that align with your core values.

Build Confidence: The more you practice saying no, the more confident you'll become in protecting your time and energy.

Step 4: Schedule Downtime

Purpose: Downtime is essential for recharging and maintaining mental clarity. By scheduling regular breaks and relaxation periods, you can prevent burnout and ensure that you have the energy to focus on your priorities.

How to Do It:

Prioritize Rest:

Schedule Regular Breaks: Incorporate short breaks into your daily routine. Whether it's a five-minute walk, a quick stretch, or a moment of deep breathing, these breaks help you recharge and maintain focus.

Plan for Leisure: Set aside time each week for activities that bring you joy and relaxation. This could be anything from reading a book to spending time in nature or enjoying a hobby.

Protect Your Downtime:

Set Boundaries: Treat your downtime as non-negotiable. Avoid letting work or other commitments encroach on this time. Communicate your boundaries clearly to others, so they understand when you're unavailable.

Unplug and Disconnect: During downtime, try to unplug from digital devices. Disconnecting from screens and technology can help you fully relax and recharge.

Incorporate Mindfulness:

Practice Mindful Relaxation: Use mindfulness techniques during downtime to enhance relaxation. Focus on your breath, engage in a mindful activity like walking or coloring, or simply sit quietly and observe your surroundings.

Reflect and Reconnect: Use some of your downtime to reflect on your progress, reconnect with your core values, and assess whether you're staying aligned with your priorities.

Create a Relaxation Routine:

Establish a Wind-Down Routine: Develop a routine that helps you transition from work or other activities into relaxation mode. This could include activities like reading, taking a warm bath, or practicing gentle stretching before bed.

Make It Consistent: Consistency is key to making downtime a regular part of your life. Aim to incorporate relaxation into your daily routine, even if it's just for a few minutes each day.

Final Thoughts:

Eliminating the non-essential is a powerful way to create space for what truly matters in your life. By identifying distractions, decluttering your environment, practicing saying no, and scheduling regular downtime, you can focus your time and energy on your core values and priorities. This intentional approach not only enhances your productivity but also brings greater clarity, balance, and fulfillment to your life.

§

Action Plan
Phase Four

Developing a Focused Mindset

Objective: The goal of this guide is to help you cultivate the mental resilience and focus needed to achieve your goals. By developing a focused mindset, you'll be better equipped to stay on track, overcome challenges, and maintain the clarity needed to reach your aspirations.

Step 1: Practice Mindfulness

Purpose: Mindfulness is a powerful tool for staying present and focused. By incorporating daily mindfulness exercises into your routine, you can train your brain to concentrate on the task at hand, reduce stress, and improve your overall mental clarity.

How to Do It:

Start with Simple Breathing Exercises:

Mindful Breathing: Begin with a basic mindful breathing exercise. Find a quiet place, sit comfortably, and close your eyes. Focus on your breath as you inhale deeply through your nose and exhale slowly through your mouth. If your mind starts to wander, gently bring your attention back to your breath. Start with just a few minutes each day and gradually increase the duration as you become more comfortable.

Counting Breaths: As you breathe, count each breath. Inhale and count "one," then exhale and count "two," continuing up to ten. If your mind drifts, start again from one. This exercise helps anchor your focus and can be particularly useful when you're feeling stressed or distracted.

Incorporate Mindfulness into Daily Activities:

Mindful Walking: Take a short walk outside and focus on each step. Pay attention to the sensation of your feet touching the ground, the rhythm of your breath, and the sounds around you. Mindful walking is a great way to bring mindfulness into your daily routine without needing extra time.

Mindful Eating: During a meal, slow down and savor each bite. Notice the textures, flavors, and aromas of your food. This practice not only enhances your enjoyment of meals but also trains your mind to stay present and focused on the moment.

Set Aside Time for Formal Mindfulness Practice:

Daily Meditation: Dedicate at least five to ten minutes each day to formal meditation. Find a quiet space where you won't be disturbed, sit comfortably, and focus on your breath or a specific mantra. Consistency is key to reaping the benefits of mindfulness, so try to practice at the same time each day.

Body Scan Meditation: Another effective mindfulness technique is the body scan. Lie down or sit comfortably and close your eyes. Slowly bring your attention to each part of your body, starting from your toes and moving up to your head. Notice any sensations, tension, or discomfort, and breathe into those areas to release any tightness.

Monitor Your Progress:

Reflect on Your Experience: At the end of each week, take a few minutes to reflect on your mindfulness practice. Notice any changes in your ability to focus, your stress levels, or your overall sense of well-being. Journaling your experiences can help track your progress and reinforce the habit.

Adjust as Needed: If you find certain exercises challenging or not particularly effective, don't hesitate to adjust your practice. The key is to find mindfulness techniques that work best for you and your lifestyle.

Step 2: Embrace Discomfort

Purpose: Growth and resilience don't happen within your comfort zone. By regularly challenging yourself with tasks outside your comfort zone, you can build mental toughness and become more adept at handling bigger challenges when they arise.

How to Do It:

Identify Areas for Growth:

Self-Assessment: Take some time to assess areas in your life where you tend to stay within your comfort zone. This could be at work, in your personal life, or in your learning experiences. Identify specific tasks or situations that make you feel uncomfortable or nervous.

Set Stretch Goals: Once you've identified these areas, set stretch goals that push you slightly beyond your current abilities. These goals should be challenging but achievable with effort. For example, if public speaking makes you uncomfortable, set a goal to speak up in a meeting or give a small presentation.

Take Small, Consistent Steps:

Start Small: Begin with manageable challenges that push you out of your comfort zone without overwhelming you. For example, if you're working on becoming more assertive, start by expressing your opinion in a low-stakes conversation.

Gradually Increase Difficulty: As you become more comfortable with smaller challenges, gradually increase the difficulty. The key is to build up your resilience incrementally, allowing your confidence to grow with each success.

Learn from Discomfort:

Reflect on Experiences: After facing a challenge, take time to reflect on what you learned from the experience. What strategies helped you succeed? What could you improve next time? Viewing discomfort as a learning opportunity can shift your mindset from one of fear to one of growth.

Celebrate Small Wins: Acknowledge and celebrate your successes, no matter how small. Each time you push through discomfort, you're building the mental toughness needed to handle even bigger challenges in the future.

Maintain a Growth Mindset:

View Challenges as Opportunities: Adopting a growth mindset means seeing challenges not as threats but as opportunities to grow. Remind yourself that every uncomfortable situation is a chance to develop new skills and build resilience.

Stay Persistent: Embracing discomfort isn't easy, and there will be times when you may feel like giving up. Stay persistent and remind yourself of the long-term benefits of pushing through your comfort zone.

Step 3: Visualize Success

Purpose: Mental imagery is a powerful tool for building resilience and focus. By visualizing yourself overcoming challenges and achieving your goals, you create a mental blueprint for success, which boosts confidence and prepares your mind to handle adversity.

How to Do It:

Create a Quiet Space:

Find a Comfortable Position: Sit or lie down in a quiet space where you won't be disturbed. Close your eyes and take a few deep breaths to center yourself.

Relax Your Body: Before beginning your visualization, take a moment to relax your body. Release any tension in your muscles, and focus on feeling calm and grounded.

Visualize Your Goals:

Picture Your Success: Imagine yourself achieving a specific goal. Visualize the steps you'll take, the obstacles you'll overcome, and the satisfaction you'll feel upon reaching your goal. Make the image as vivid as possible, including sights, sounds, and emotions.

Focus on the Process: Don't just visualize the end result—focus on the process that will get you there. See yourself working through challenges, staying focused, and using your skills and resources effectively.

Use Positive Affirmations:

Incorporate Affirmations: As you visualize your success, use positive affirmations to reinforce your confidence. For example, repeat phrases like, "I am capable of overcoming any challenge," or "I have the strength and focus to achieve my goals."

Believe in Your Success: As you visualize, focus on believing in your ability to succeed. The more you practice this, the more your mind will accept it as reality, which can significantly boost your confidence and resilience.

Practice Regularly:

Daily Visualization: Make visualization a daily practice, even if it's just for a few minutes. The more you practice, the more natural and effective it will become.

Adapt as Needed: As your goals evolve, update your visualizations to reflect your current objectives and challenges. This keeps the practice relevant and aligned with your growth.

Step 4: Set Achievable Goals

Purpose: Setting small, achievable goals helps you build confidence and momentum, making it easier to tackle larger challenges. Breaking down bigger goals into manageable tasks ensures that you stay focused and motivated throughout your journey.

How to Do It:

Break Down Larger Goals:

Identify Your Main Goal: Start by identifying a larger goal you want to achieve. This could be something like completing a project at work, developing a new skill, or improving your health.

Divide Into Smaller Tasks: Break down your main goal into smaller, manageable tasks. For example, if your goal is to write a book, your smaller tasks might include outlining chapters, writing for a set amount of time each day, and editing sections weekly.

Set SMART Goals:

Specific: Ensure each task is clear and specific. Instead of saying, "Work on the project," specify what you'll do, such as "Complete the first draft of the introduction."

Measurable: Define how you'll measure progress. For instance, "Write 500 words today" is a measurable goal.

Achievable: Set goals that are challenging yet attainable given your current resources and time.

Relevant: Ensure each task contributes to your larger goal and aligns with your core values.

Time-Bound: Assign a deadline to each task. This creates a sense of urgency and helps keep you on track.

Monitor Progress and Adjust:

Track Your Progress: Keep a record of your achievements. This could be a simple checklist, a journal, or a digital tracker. Seeing your progress builds confidence and reinforces your commitment.

Adjust as Needed: If you encounter obstacles, don't be afraid to adjust your goals. The key is to stay flexible and adapt your plan as you learn more about what works and what doesn't.

Celebrate Small Wins:

Acknowledge Achievements: Celebrate each small victory along the way. Whether it's finishing a chapter, completing a workout, or reaching a milestone, acknowledging these wins boosts morale and motivates you to keep going.

Reflect on Growth: Take time to reflect on how each small achievement contributes to your overall growth. This reflection helps reinforce the importance of persistence and effort.

Final Thoughts:

Developing a focused mindset is crucial for achieving your goals and living a life aligned with your core values. By practicing mindfulness, embracing discomfort, visualizing success, and setting achievable goals, you'll build the mental resilience and focus needed to overcome challenges and stay on track. These steps not only help you achieve your goals but also create a solid foundation for ongoing personal growth and fulfillment.

Action Plan
Phase Five

Creating Effective Routines

Objective: The goal of this guide is to help you establish daily routines that align with your core values and support a life focused on what truly matters. By designing effective routines, you can create a structured environment that fosters productivity, mindfulness, and overall well-being.

Step 1: Design Morning and Evening Routines

Purpose: Morning and evening routines are crucial for setting the tone for your day and ensuring a restful, reflective end to it. These routines help you start the day with intention and close it with a sense of accomplishment and peace.

How to Do It:

Morning Routine: Start Your Day with Purpose

Wake Up Early: Start by setting a consistent wake-up time that allows you enough space to ease into the day. Waking up early provides a quiet, uninterrupted time to focus on yourself before the demands of the day begin.

Hydrate and Nourish: Begin your morning by drinking a glass of water to rehydrate your body. Follow it up with a nutritious breakfast that fuels your body and mind for the day ahead.

Mindful Movement: Incorporate some form of physical activity, whether it's stretching, yoga, or a brisk walk. This helps energize your body and boosts your mood.

Set Intentions: Take a few minutes to set your intentions for the day. This could involve writing down your top three priorities, visualizing a successful day, or practicing gratitude for what lies ahead.

Focus on Personal Growth: Spend 15-30 minutes on activities that contribute to your personal growth, such as reading, journaling, or learning something new. This practice reinforces your commitment to continuous improvement and sets a positive tone for the day.

Evening Routine: Wind Down and Reflect

Disconnect from Technology: At least an hour before bed, turn off screens and devices. This reduces exposure to blue light, which can interfere with sleep, and helps your mind unwind from the day's activities.

Review the Day: Take a few minutes to reflect on your day. What did you accomplish? What challenges did you face? What are you grateful for? This reflection helps you end the day on a positive note and prepares you for tomorrow.

Plan for Tomorrow: Write down any tasks or goals for the next day. This helps clear your mind of any lingering thoughts or worries, allowing you to relax more easily.

Relaxation Routine: Engage in a relaxing activity before bed, such as reading, meditating, or taking a warm bath. This helps signal to your body that it's time to wind down and prepares you for restful sleep.

Consistency is Key:

Stick to Your Routines: The effectiveness of routines comes from consistency. Try to stick to your morning and evening routines as closely as possible, even on weekends or holidays. The more consistent you are, the more these routines will become second nature, setting you up for success each day.

Step 2: Incorporate Reflection Time

Purpose: Regular reflection is essential for staying aligned with your goals and values. By dedicating time to reflect on what's working and what needs adjustment, you can continuously improve your routines and overall approach to life.

How to Do It:

Daily Reflection:

End-of-Day Review: Set aside five to ten minutes at the end of each day to reflect on your experiences. Consider what went well, what challenges you faced, and what you learned. This daily check-in helps you stay mindful of your progress and areas for improvement.

Journal Your Thoughts: Writing down your reflections in a journal can provide valuable insights over time. You can track patterns, notice changes in your mindset, and celebrate your growth.

Weekly Reflection:

Weekly Review Session: At the end of each week, schedule a more in-depth reflection session. Review your goals, assess your progress, and identify any adjustments needed. This is also a good time to plan for the upcoming week and ensure your routines are still aligned with your priorities.

Celebrate Wins: Take time to acknowledge and celebrate your achievements, no matter how small. This reinforces positive behavior and keeps you motivated.

Monthly Reflection:

Assess Long-Term Goals: Each month, take a step back to reflect on your long-term goals and how your daily and weekly actions are contributing to them. This broader perspective helps you stay on track and make necessary adjustments to your routines.

Step 3: Use the Pomodoro Technique

Purpose: The Pomodoro Technique is a time management method that helps you maintain focus and productivity by working in short, focused bursts followed by regular breaks. This technique is especially useful for avoiding burnout and ensuring sustained concentration.

How to Do It:

Set Up Your Work Sessions:

Choose a Task: Select a specific task to work on during your Pomodoro session. Break down larger tasks into smaller, manageable parts if necessary.

Set a Timer: Set a timer for 25 minutes. During this time, focus solely on the task at hand. Avoid multitasking or distractions.

Work in Focused Bursts:

Work for 25 Minutes: Concentrate on your task for the full 25 minutes. If a distracting thought or task comes to mind, jot it down to address later but stay focused on your current work.

Take a Short Break: Once the timer goes off, take a 5-minute break. Use this time to stretch, walk around, or do something relaxing.

Repeat the Cycle:

Complete Four Pomodoros: After four Pomodoro sessions (25 minutes of work followed by 5 minutes of break), take a longer break of 15-30 minutes. This allows you to recharge before starting the next cycle.

Adjust Based on Your Needs: If 25-minute sessions don't work for you, adjust the duration. The key is to find a balance that maximizes your productivity without causing fatigue.

Track Your Progress:

Record Completed Pomodoros: Keep track of how many Pomodoros you complete in a day. This can help you measure your productivity and identify patterns in your focus and energy levels.

Reflect on Efficiency: At the end of the day or week, review your Pomodoro sessions to see where you were most productive and where you struggled. Use this information to adjust your approach as needed.

Step 4: Integrate Mindful Breathing

Purpose: Mindful breathing exercises are a simple yet powerful way to manage stress, stay calm, and maintain focus throughout the day. By integrating mindful breathing into your routine, you can improve your ability to stay centered and resilient under pressure.

How to Do It:

Learn the Basics of Mindful Breathing:

Focus on Your Breath: Sit comfortably, close your eyes, and focus on your breath. Notice the sensation of the air as it enters and leaves your body. If your mind starts to wander, gently bring your attention back to your breath.

Count Your Breaths: Inhale deeply through your nose for a count of four, hold your breath for a count of four, then exhale slowly through your mouth for a count of four. Repeat this cycle for several minutes.

Incorporate Breathing into Your Daily Routine:

Start Your Day with Breathing Exercises: Begin your morning routine with a few minutes of mindful breathing. This helps set a calm and focused tone for the day.

Use Breathing to Manage Stress: Whenever you feel stressed or overwhelmed, pause and take a few deep, mindful breaths. This can help reduce stress hormones and bring your mind back to the present moment.

Practice Breathing Before Important Tasks:

Prepare for Meetings or Presentations: Before a meeting, presentation, or challenging task, take a few moments to practice mindful breathing. This helps calm your nerves and sharpen your focus.

End Your Day with Breathing Exercises: Incorporate a brief breathing exercise into your evening routine to help you wind down and prepare for restful sleep.

Monitor the Effects:

Track Your Calmness Levels: Pay attention to how mindful breathing affects your mood, focus, and stress levels. Keep a journal to note any changes or patterns.

Adjust Your Practice: If you notice that certain breathing techniques work better for you, adjust your practice accordingly. The goal is to make mindful breathing a natural and effective part of your routine.

Final Thoughts:

Creating effective routines is a powerful way to bring structure, focus, and intentionality into your life. By designing morning and evening routines, incorporating regular reflection, using the Pomodoro

Technique, and integrating mindful breathing, you can establish a daily rhythm that supports your goals and enhances your well-being. These routines will help you stay on track, manage stress, and make consist

§

Action Plan
Phase Six

Staying Grounded in Your Purpose

Objective: The goal of this guide is to help you remain connected to your core values and long-term goals, even when faced with challenges. By staying grounded in your purpose, you ensure that your actions and decisions consistently align with what truly matters to you, fostering resilience and sustained motivation.

Step 1: Regular Reflection

Purpose: Regular reflection allows you to assess your progress, evaluate your current path, and make necessary adjustments. This practice helps you stay aligned with your core values and ensures that your daily actions are contributing to your long-term goals.

How to Do It:

Schedule Weekly Reflection Time:

Set a Consistent Time: Choose a specific day and time each week dedicated to reflection. This could be at the end of your workweek or during a quiet moment on the weekend. The key is to make this time non-negotiable.

Create a Comfortable Environment: Find a peaceful space where you can focus without distractions. Consider using a journal, reflection prompts, or meditation to help guide your thoughts.

Review Your Week:

Assess Progress: Reflect on the goals you set for the week. Did you achieve them? What contributed to your success or prevented you from reaching them? This assessment helps you understand what's working and what isn't.

Identify Challenges: Consider any obstacles or challenges you faced during the week. How did you respond? What could you do differently next time? Reflecting on challenges helps you learn and grow from each experience.

Reaffirm Your Values: Take a moment to reconnect with your core values. Ask yourself if your actions and decisions this week were in line with these values. If not, identify areas where you can make adjustments.

Plan for the Week Ahead:

Set New Goals: Based on your reflection, set specific, achievable goals for the upcoming week. Ensure these goals align with your long-term vision and core values.

Adjust Your Approach: If you identified any areas for improvement, plan how you will address them in the coming week. This might involve changing your routines, setting new priorities, or adopting a different mindset.

End with Gratitude:

Express Gratitude: Conclude your reflection session by acknowledging the positive aspects of your week. Expressing gratitude helps you stay grounded in the present and appreciate the journey, not just the destination.

Step 2: Reconnect with Your 'Why'

Purpose: Your 'why' is the underlying reason behind your goals and actions. Regularly reconnecting with your 'why' ensures that you remain motivated and aligned with your purpose, especially during challenging times.

How to Do It:

Clarify Your 'Why':

Identify Your Motivations: Reflect on the deeper reasons behind your goals. Why are these goals important to you? What values do they reflect? Understanding your motivations provides clarity and direction.

Write It Down: Document your 'why' in a journal or on a vision board. Having a physical reminder of your purpose makes it easier to stay connected to it, especially when you face setbacks.

Integrate Your 'Why' into Daily Life:

Start Your Day with Purpose: Each morning, take a moment to remind yourself of your 'why'. This could be through a brief meditation, reading your written statement, or visualizing the impact of achieving your goals.

Use Affirmations: Incorporate affirmations related to your 'why' into your daily routine. Repeating these affirmations helps reinforce your commitment and keeps your purpose at the forefront of your mind.

Check In Regularly:

Weekly or Monthly Review: In addition to your regular reflection, take time to revisit your 'why' on a weekly or monthly basis. Ask yourself if it still resonates with you and if your actions are aligned with it. If necessary, refine your 'why' to reflect any changes in your values or circumstances.

Lean on Your 'Why' During Tough Times:

Motivation During Challenges: When you encounter obstacles, remind yourself of your 'why'. Understanding the bigger picture helps you push through difficulties and maintain resilience.

Step 3: Celebrate Small Wins

Purpose: Celebrating small wins is essential for maintaining motivation and building momentum. Recognizing and appreciating your progress, no matter how small, keeps you motivated and reinforces the positive behaviors that lead to success.

How to Do It:

Identify Small Wins:

Define What Counts: Recognize that progress comes in many forms. Small wins could include completing a challenging task, maintaining a positive habit, or overcoming a minor setback. These achievements are all steps toward your larger goals.

Acknowledge Progress: At the end of each day or week, take a moment to identify the small wins you've achieved. Write them down in a journal or share them with a trusted friend or mentor.

Celebrate in Meaningful Ways:

Personal Rewards: Celebrate your small wins in a way that feels meaningful to you. This could be as simple as treating yourself to a favorite snack, taking a relaxing break, or enjoying a hobby you love. The key is to acknowledge your progress in a way that reinforces your commitment to your goals.

Share Your Success: Sharing your wins with others can enhance your sense of accomplishment. Consider sharing your progress with a supportive community, accountability partner, or mentor who can celebrate with you and offer encouragement.

Use Wins as Building Blocks:

Build Momentum: Recognize that each small win is a building block toward your larger goals. Use the momentum from these wins to propel you forward and tackle the next challenge.

Reflect on Wins During Tough Times: When you face difficulties, revisit your small wins. Reflecting on past successes can boost your confidence and remind you that progress is possible, even when the path seems challenging.

Create a Win Journal:

Document Your Journey: Consider keeping a dedicated journal to document your small wins. Over time, this journal becomes a powerful reminder of your growth and progress, providing inspiration whenever you need it.

Final Thoughts:

Staying grounded in your purpose is essential for living a life aligned with your values and goals. By incorporating regular reflection, reconnecting with your 'why,' and celebrating small wins, you can maintain a strong sense of direction and motivation, even in the face of challenges. These practices help you stay focused on what truly matters, ensuring that your journey is as meaningful as your destination.

§

Action Plan
Phase Seven

Building a Legacy

Objective: The goal of this guide is to help you create a life that leaves a positive, lasting impact on others and the world around you. Building a legacy involves intentional living, aligning your actions with your values, and contributing to something greater than yourself.

Step 1: Identify Your Desired Legacy

Purpose: Understanding the legacy you want to leave is the foundation of living a life of purpose. By clearly defining how you want to be remembered and the impact you wish to have, you can ensure your daily actions are meaningful and aligned with your long-term vision.

How to Do It:

Reflect on Your Values and Impact:

Clarify Core Values: Begin by revisiting your core values. These are the principles that define who you are and what you stand for. Consider how these values can shape the legacy you want to leave.

Visualize Your Legacy: Take time to visualize the impact you want to have on others and the world. How do you want to be remembered by your family, friends, colleagues, and community? What contributions do you want to be known for?

Consider Your Passions and Strengths: Reflect on your passions, talents, and strengths. How can you use these to make a difference in the lives of others? Identifying your unique contributions will help you define a legacy that is both authentic and impactful.

Write a Legacy Statement:

Create a Personal Mission Statement: Write a brief statement that encapsulates the legacy you wish to leave. This could include your values, the impact you want to have, and the ways you plan to achieve it. Having a written statement serves as a constant reminder of your long-term goals.

Reflect on Your Legacy Statement Regularly: Review your legacy statement regularly to ensure it still resonates with you. As you grow and evolve, your vision for your legacy may also change. Adjust your statement as needed to reflect your current values and goals.

Step 2: Align Actions with Legacy Goals

Purpose: Once you've identified your desired legacy, the next step is to align your daily actions with your legacy goals. This ensures that every decision you make contributes to the lasting impact you wish to create.

How to Do It:

Set Legacy-Focused Goals:

Break Down Your Legacy into Achievable Goals: Identify specific, actionable goals that contribute to your legacy. These could be personal, professional, or community-focused goals that align with your vision.

Prioritize Actions that Support Your Legacy: Use tools like the Eisenhower Matrix or time blocking to prioritize tasks and actions that directly contribute to your legacy. Ensure that these priorities are reflected in your daily, weekly, and monthly plans.

Make Decisions with Your Legacy in Mind:

Evaluate Your Choices: Before making decisions, ask yourself if the choice aligns with the legacy you want to leave. Consider the long-term impact of your actions on others and on your legacy.

Stay Consistent: Consistency is key to building a legacy. Ensure that your actions, both big and small, are consistently aligned with your legacy goals. This builds trust and reinforces the impact you wish to have.

Create Habits that Support Your Legacy:

Develop Positive Habits: Identify habits that will help you achieve your legacy goals. For example, if your legacy involves mentoring others, develop a habit of regularly offering guidance and support to those around you.

Eliminate Habits that Detract from Your Legacy: Reflect on any habits or behaviors that might undermine your legacy goals. Work on gradually eliminating these habits to ensure your actions consistently contribute to your desired impact.

Step 3: Share Your Journey

Purpose: Sharing your journey with others not only amplifies your impact but also inspires and empowers others to contribute to your legacy. Mentoring, storytelling, and active involvement in your community can help you create a ripple effect that extends beyond your immediate circle.

How to Do It:

Mentor and Teach Others:

Identify Opportunities to Mentor: Seek out opportunities to mentor others in your area of expertise or passion. This could be through formal mentoring programs, community organizations, or informal relationships.

Share Your Knowledge and Experience: Be open about your journey, including both successes and failures. Sharing your insights and lessons learned can help others grow and contribute to the legacy you're building.

Engage with Your Community:

Contribute to Causes Aligned with Your Values: Get involved in causes or organizations that align with your legacy goals. This could involve volunteering, donating, or advocating for issues that matter to you.

Participate in Community Building: Engage in activities that strengthen your community, such as organizing events, leading initiatives, or supporting local leaders. Community involvement reinforces the positive impact you want to leave.

Document Your Journey:

Write or Speak About Your Legacy: Consider writing a blog, book, or series of articles that document your journey and share your vision with a broader audience. Public speaking or leading workshops are also effective ways to spread your message.

Create a Legacy Project: Consider creating a tangible project that embodies your legacy, such as establishing a scholarship fund, launching a community initiative, or starting a foundation. These projects can serve as lasting reminders of your impact.

Step 4: Continue Learning and Growing

Purpose: Building a legacy is an ongoing process that requires continuous learning, adaptation, and personal growth. Committing to lifelong learning ensures that your legacy remains relevant and impactful over time.

How to Do It:

Commit to Lifelong Learning:

Pursue Ongoing Education: Continuously seek out opportunities to learn and grow, whether through formal education, reading, attending workshops, or engaging with new ideas. Staying informed and open to new perspectives enhances your ability to adapt and contribute meaningfully to your legacy.

Embrace New Challenges: Regularly challenge yourself with new experiences, skills, or knowledge areas. Embracing challenges fosters personal growth and keeps you motivated to contribute to your legacy.

Adapt to Change:

Stay Flexible: Understand that your legacy may evolve as you grow and as the world changes. Be open to refining your vision and adapting your actions to ensure that your legacy remains relevant and impactful.

Seek Feedback and Reflection: Regularly seek feedback from others and reflect on your progress. Use this input to adjust your approach and continue growing in alignment with your legacy goals.

Incorporate New Insights into Your Legacy:

Apply What You Learn: As you acquire new knowledge and skills, find ways to incorporate these insights into your legacy-building efforts. This could involve adopting new practices, changing your approach, or expanding your impact in new areas.

Mentor the Next Generation: As you continue learning, share your newfound knowledge with others, particularly younger generations. Helping others grow ensures that your legacy extends beyond your lifetime.

Final Thoughts:

Building a legacy is about more than just the impact you leave behind; it's about living a life of purpose, intention, and continuous growth. By identifying your desired legacy, aligning your actions with your goals, sharing your journey, and committing to lifelong learning, you can create a lasting, positive impact that resonates with others and continues to grow long after you're gone.

§

Appendix - B

Suggestions for Further Exploration

Listed by Action Plan Phases

Clarify Your Core Values

"The 7 Habits of Highly Effective People" by Stephen R. Covey. Covey's book is a cornerstone in personal development, providing a deep dive into identifying and living by your core values. The principles discussed align well with the process of clarifying and prioritizing core values.

"Dare to Lead" by Brené Brown. Brené Brown explores the importance of vulnerability, courage, and living according to one's values in leadership and life. This book is excellent for understanding how core values influence decision-making and leadership.

Set Your Life Priorities

"Essentialism: The Disciplined Pursuit of Less" by Greg McKeown McKeown's book teaches the importance of focusing on what truly matters, making it a perfect companion for setting and aligning your life priorities with your core values.

"Atomic Habits: An Easy & Proven Way to Build Good Habits & Break Bad Ones" by James Clear. This book provides practical strategies for building habits that align with your priorities, helping you focus on what's most important in your life.

Eliminate the Non-Essential

"The Life-Changing Magic of Tidying Up" by Marie Kondo. Kondo's book is a practical guide to decluttering your physical environment, which is a key step in eliminating non-essential distractions in your life.

"Deep Work: Rules for Focused Success in a Distracted World" by Cal Newport. Newport's book offers strategies for eliminating digital distractions and creating an environment conducive to focused, meaningful work.

Develop a Focused Mindset

"Grit: The Power of Passion and Perseverance" by Angela Duckworth. Duckworth's exploration of grit—sustained passion and perseverance for long-term goals—provides valuable insights into developing a resilient and focused mindset.

"Mindset: The New Psychology of Success" by Carol S. Dweck. Dweck's book on the growth mindset is essential for understanding how to cultivate a mindset that embraces challenges and focuses on continuous improvement.

Create Effective Routines

"The Miracle Morning" by Hal Elrod. Elrod's book outlines a morning routine designed to set a positive and focused tone for the day, making it a valuable resource for those looking to establish effective daily routines.

"Atomic Habits: An Easy & Proven Way to Build Good Habits & Break Bad Ones" by James Clear. Clear's book offers actionable strategies for creating and maintaining habits that support effective routines.

Stay Grounded in Your Purpose

"Man's Search for Meaning" by Viktor E. Frankl. Frankl's exploration of finding purpose and meaning, even in the face of extreme adversity, offers profound insights into staying grounded in your purpose.

"Start with Why: How Great Leaders Inspire Everyone to Take Action" by Simon Sinek. Sinek's book emphasizes the importance of understanding your deeper purpose, which is crucial for staying connected to your core values and long-term goals.

Build a Legacy

"The 7 Habits of Highly Effective People" by Stephen R. Covey Covey's classic book offers foundational strategies for building a life and legacy focused on long-term impact and core values.

"The 5 AM Club: Own Your Morning, Elevate Your Life" by Robin Sharma. Sharma's book provides insights on how daily discipline and intentional living can contribute to leaving a lasting legacy.

Bibliography

Allen, D. (2001). Getting things done: The art of stress-free productivity. Penguin Books.

Amabile, T. M., & Kramer, S. J. (2011). The progress principle: Using small wins to ignite joy, engagement, and creativity at work. Harvard Business Review Press.

Anderson, B. A., Laurent, P. A., & Yantis, S. (2011). Value-driven attentional capture. Proceedings of the National Academy of Sciences, 108(25), 10367-10371.

Bandura, A. (1977). Social learning theory. Prentice Hall.

Baumeister, R. F., & Tierney, J. (2011). Willpower: Rediscovering the greatest human strength. Penguin Press.

Baumeister, R. F., Bratslavsky, E., Muraven, M., & Tice, D. M. (2000). Ego depletion: Is the active self a limited resource? Journal of Personality and Social Psychology, 74(5), 1252-1265.

Becker, J. (2013). Clutterfree with kids. Becoming Minimalist Press.

Brown, B. (2010). The gifts of imperfection: Let go of who you think you're supposed to be and embrace who you are. Hazelden Publishing.

Brown, B. (2018). Dare to lead: Brave work. Tough conversations. Whole hearts. Random House.

Buzan, T. (2006). The mind map book: Unlock your creativity, boost your memory, change your life. BBC Active.

Chapman, G. (1995). The five love languages: The secret to love that lasts. Northfield Publishing.

Cirillo, F. (2006). The Pomodoro Technique. FC Garage.

Clear, J. (2018). Atomic habits: An easy & proven way to build good habits & break bad ones. Avery.

Cloud, H., & Townsend, J. (1992). Boundaries: When to say yes, how to say no to take control of your life. Zondervan.

Covey, S. R. (1989). The 7 habits of highly effective people: Powerful lessons in personal change. Free Press.

Csikszentmihalyi, M. (1990). Flow: The psychology of optimal experience. Harper & Row.

Deci, E. L., & Ryan, R. M. (2000). The "what" and "why" of goal pursuits: Human needs and the self-determination of behavior. Psychological Inquiry, 11(4), 227-268.

Duhigg, C. (2012). The power of habit: Why we do what we do in life and business. Random House.

Dunbar, R. I. M. (1992). Neocortex size as a constraint on group size in primates. Journal of Human Evolution, 22(6), 469-493.

Dweck, C. S. (2006). Mindset: The new psychology of success. Random House.

Eisenhower, D. D. (1954). Speech to the Second Assembly of the World Council of Churches. Evanston, Illinois.

Elrod, H. (2012). The miracle morning: The not-so-obvious secret guaranteed to transform your life (before 8AM). Hal Elrod International.

Franklin, B. (1791). The autobiography of Benjamin Franklin. J. Parson.

Gawande, A. (2010). The checklist manifesto: How to get things right. Metropolitan Books.

Gollwitzer, P. M. (1999). Implementation intentions: Strong effects of simple plans. American Psychologist, 54(7), 493-503.

Gollwitzer, P. M., & Sheeran, P. (2006). Implementation intentions and goal achievement: A meta-analysis of effects and processes. Advances in Experimental Social Psychology, 38, 69-119.

Goleman, D. (1995). Emotional intelligence: Why it can matter more than IQ. Bantam Books.

González, V. M., & Mark, G. (2004). "Constant, constant, multi-tasking craziness": Managing multiple working spheres. In Proceedings of the SIGCHI Conference on Human Factors in Computing Systems (pp. 113-120).

Gottman, J. M., & Silver, N. (1999). The seven principles for making marriage work. Crown Publishing Group.

Isaacson, W. (2011). Steve Jobs. Simon & Schuster.

Kabat-Zinn, J. (1994). Wherever you go, there you are: Mindfulness meditation in everyday life. Hyperion.

Kolb, D. A. (1984). Experiential learning: Experience as the source of learning and development. Prentice-Hall.

Koch, R. (1998). The 80/20 principle: The secret to achieving more with less. Crown Business.

Locke, E. A., & Latham, G. P. (2002). Building a practically useful theory of goal setting and task motivation: A 35-year odyssey. American Psychologist, 57(9), 705-717.

Lyubomirsky, S., King, L., & Diener, E. (2005). The benefits of frequent positive affect: Does happiness lead to success? Psychological Bulletin, 131(6), 803-855.

McKeown, G. (2014). Essentialism: The disciplined pursuit of less. Crown Business.

Miller, G. A. (1956). The magical number seven, plus or minus two: Some limits on our capacity for processing information. Psychological Review, 63(2), 81-97.

Newport, C. (2016). Deep work: Rules for focused success in a distracted world. Grand Central Publishing.

Newport, C. (2019). Digital minimalism: Choosing a focused life in a noisy world. Portfolio.

Nobel Prize. (2014). The Nobel Peace Prize 2014 – Press release. Retrieved from https://www.nobelprize.org/prizes/peace/2014/press-release/

Pink, D. H. (2009). Drive: The surprising truth about what motivates us. Riverhead Books.

Pronk, N. P., & Righart, R. (2016). The power of connection: Building a culture of health through positive relationships and social networks. American Journal of Health Promotion, 30(5), 388-389.

Reis, H. T., & Shaver, P. (1988). Intimacy as an interpersonal process. In S. Duck (Ed.), Handbook of personal relationships (pp. 367-389). Wiley.

Rokeach, M. (1973). The nature of human values. Free Press.

Rosen, C. (2008). The myth of multitasking. The New Atlantis, 20, 105-110.

Schein, E. H. (2010). Organizational culture and leadership (4th ed.). Jossey-Bass.

Schon, D. A. (1983). The reflective practitioner: How professionals think in action. Basic Books.

Schwartz, S. H. (2012). An overview of the Schwartz theory of basic values. Online Readings in Psychology and Culture, 2(1).

Senge, P. M. (1990). The fifth discipline: The art & practice of the learning organization. Doubleday.

Sinek, S. (2009). Start with why: How great leaders inspire everyone to take action. Penguin Books.

Steel, P. (2007). The nature of procrastination: A meta-analytic and theoretical review of quintessential self-regulatory failure. Psychological Bulletin, 133(1), 65-94.

Turkle, S. (2015). Reclaiming conversation: The power of talk in a digital age. Penguin Press.

Vance, A. (2015). Elon Musk: Tesla, SpaceX, and the quest for a fantastic future. Ecco.

Vohs, K. D., Redden, J. P., & Rahinel, R. (2013). Physical order produces healthy choices, generosity, and conventionality, whereas disorder produces creativity. Psychological Science, 24(9), 1860-1867.

‡ ‡ ‡

Index